Two Skis and a Rifle: An Introduction to Biathlon

Michael P Nordvall

Cover Artwork (Biathlete vector artwork mage by Michal Sanca/ Shutterstock.com)

Two Skis and a Rifle: An Introduction to Biathlon

Michael P Nordvall

Published by Michael P Nordvall, 2024.

While every precaution has been taken in the preparation of this book, the publisher assumes no responsibility for errors or omissions, or for damages resulting from the use of the information contained herein.

TWO SKIS AND A RIFLE: AN INTRODUCTION TO BIATHLON

First edition. April 8, 2024.

Copyright © 2024 Michael P Nordvall.

ISBN: 978-1393231349

Written by Michael P Nordvall.

Table of Contents

Introduction 1

Chapter One | From Military Beginnings 7

Chapter Two | To the Sport of Biathlon 17

Chapter Three | Venues and Events 29

Chapter Four | On Being a World Class Biathlete 55

Chapter Five | Skiing: From Technology to Technique, it's Half the Battle 81

Chapter Six | Going Clean 103

Chapter Seven | Competing Clean Means Year-Round Training 127

Epilogue 153

Bibliography and Notes 162

Dedication

This book would only be made possible through the generosity of family and friends. I would first like to thank my wife Tish for her enduring support and encouragement throughout the process of my writing from conception to completion; you kept me going day after day. Thank you to my family for simply asking how the writing was progressing and to my mother Helen and mother-in-law Jolly for their editorial feedback and suggestions despite having little prior exposure to biathlon. I am indebted to my friends and colleagues at Marymount University who took on whatever little slack I may have left behind during my four month absence. And without the support of Marymount University who granted the sabbatical to undertake this work, this book never would have been completed let alone started.

Introduction

Biathlon, the Olympic endeavor that simultaneously combines precision rifle marksmanship under the duress of cross-country skiing, is the most popular European televised spectator sport during winter months. With roots in Norwegian and global military history, the sport has blossomed from high latitude training exercises into a modern annual World Cup season that crowns individuals and nations alike as world champions in competition disciplines ranging from team relays to individually timed endurance events. During the 2016/2017 season, the United States had its best ever performance on the elite World Cup circuit, placing two individuals, Susan Dunklee and Lowell Bailey, in the medals at the yearly World Championships, the single most important event in the sport other than the Winter Olympic Games. Dunklee would go on to match her performance at the 2020 Italian World Championships in the sprint race. Since their retirement, a slew of rising American hopefuls are giving their all to represent the United States on the World Cup Biathlon circuit. Perhaps it is a juxtaposition of exporting the sport of biathlon from Europe to America rather than being a form of mandatory in some cases military service or training that has precluded an American from medaling in the early 'Military Patrol' or modern versions of this winter Olympic spectacle. After winning medals at every level of competition during the 2019/2020 season, the future does look bright for the United States with U.S. Biathlon, the governing body of the sport in the Unites States, having gone so far as to import experienced head coaches of Norwegian and Italian heritage to guide our athletes to new heights.

To understand the emergence of Olympic biathlon, the pinnacle of competition in the sport, and the World Cup season is to recount the military foundation on which the sport stands. Set primarily in Europe, with occasional incursions to North America, events are held at Nordic skiing arenas with permanent shooting ranges and athlete facilities. The life of a biathlete is one of travel, training, and competing under the national flag of their home country and would be impossible without considerable personnel and budgetary support. And while certain nations have larger budgets and resources than others, the playing field is leveled once boots are clipped to skis and the rifle is harnessed to the back.

The story of biathlon begins "From Military Beginnings" and highlights major utilization of ski warfare from early Scandinavia and Russia to World Wars I and II and is interspersed with smaller tales of espionage and military tactics which are still employed today. Certainly, the portrayals of ski warfare in chapter one are not complete historical recreations nor are all political ramifications considered but rather attempt to provide insight on how militarization and tactical use of winter infantry necessitated the use of skis and weapons. As a result, training exercises for ski warfare were the norm in places like Norway, Finland, and Russia and became the precursor to the sport of biathlon as we know it today.

The evolution of biathlon as a sport which followed in the footsteps of ski warfare is discussed in chapter two. Biathlon in its present form seceded from early Pentathlon to become a standalone Olympic sport in 1960 after undergoing major organizational and structural shifts. Several innovations shaped the sport and are briefly discussed here, and in much greater detail in later chapters, including the type of rifle used in demonstrating marksmanship, target technology, and approach/style of skiing which evolved from classic or diagonal stride to contemporary skating technique. Along the way, competitions were redesigned and new races were introduced as the sport matured and grew in popularity.

TWO SKIS AND A RIFLE: AN INTRODUCTION TO BIATHLON

Chapter three has two overarching goals, 1) to introduce the reader to recurring biathlon venues and, 2) to analyze the different types of races currently run on the World Cup biathlon program. Many of the venues highlighted in this chapter will appear again in subsequent seasons with several exceptions that are mentioned in the afterword. During the upcoming Winter Olympics in Milano Cortina, Italy, the reader can expect to see no fewer than eleven individual and team relay biathlon events for both men and women, the newest being the single mixed relay. And while not all races are held at every World Cup venue, save for the World Championships, the reader should gain insight on the structure of particular races to include distances skied and shooting requirements as well as tidbits about the host venue. Tales from select competitions will conceivably impart an excitement that surrounds this extremely popular and primarily European sport. Action from races and even full race replays mentioned in this and other chapters may be found online through video streaming applications and services such as YouTube or the website of the governing body of World Cup Biathlon; the International Biathlon Union (IBU).

Chapter Four views the life of a world class biathlete from the outside looking in and attempts to provide perspective on how these athletes qualify to participate in races at the highest level, which would not be possible without strong team support. Few elite biathletes will retire on their winnings or stipends from national federations, and many hold down a second job whenever possible in the off-season to supplement income. Yet most do it out of love for the sport which is appreciated by fans who embrace this blue-collar pastime and their heroic national athletes. Ascending to the top of the sport doesn't always go smoothly, and this chapter explores an occurrence when the race jury was forced into deciding the outcome of a race. Biathletes themselves have heroes, current or former peers on the World Cup or Olympic scenes that possess(ed) a certain extra quality that cemented their status as a legend of the sport. Chapter four concludes with brief biographies of these legendary biathletes considered by many to be the greatest of all time.

Skiing is half the battle in biathlon and chapter five reminisces on the history of Nordic skiing and how advances in ski and binding technology instigated an evolution in skiing technique. A great challenge of any national teams' waxing technicians is to find the right combination of ski waxes for the day which is largely dependent on snow and environmental conditions. The single most influential advance in waxing technology had been the advent of fluorocarbon (fluor) waxes which improved almost overnight the performance of Nordic skiers and biathletes alike. Yet a new challenge has emerged for ski wax technicians following the IBU's decision to ban the use of fluor wax for the 2023/24 season and beyond in the wake of environmental and safety concerns. Waiting now for their skis to be delivered by a wax technician, biathletes will already be engrossed in their pre-race routine of equipment checks and warm-ups as the race draws near.

Perhaps the least understood aspect of biathlon to the casual observer is the connection of rifle marksmanship with skiing. Chapter six begins with an anatomical analysis of the .22 LR rifle used in competition and how biathletes add their own touches to this precision instrument. Aiming is as much an art as it is a well-choreographed routine of getting into and out of prone and standing shooting positions. Fortunately, to ensure accuracy of shooting, biathletes are given the opportunity to 'zero' in their rifles prior to the start of every race which helps to avoid trips around a penalty loop or time penalties for missed shots. To further assist a biathlete on the shooting range, coaches provide real time information on shot groupings which is relayed to an athlete out on the course. Statistics on the shooting performance of top biathletes provide benchmark data for rival competitors and rounds out the discussion on 'going clean'.

The physiological demands of biathlon are enormous and without proper year-round training, chances of success are slim to none. Talent alone will only take an athlete so far, and living the life of a biathlete means that there really isn't an off-season. Chapter seven explores how teams have solved the conundrum of training in the summer when snow has long disappeared in most regions of the world. Simulating skiing in the summer, shooting drills, frequent physiological testing, and traveling to training camps are typical for athletes as national federations have adopted modern periodization training techniques. Interestingly in this close-knit sport, athletes from rival nations will often be seen congenially training alongside one another at locations that uniquely cater to biathletes. And as with most endurance sports, biathlon has not been immune to controversy surrounding unethical practices of doping, yet the sport by-and-large remains relatively clean as athletes are subject to strict anti-doping control and adhere to self-imposed high ethical standards.

This book is written from the perspective of a biathlon fan by avocation and Professor of Health and Human Performance by profession using a variety of sources to elucidate the complexities of the sport and life of an elite biathlete. There is a decidedly American slant to the writing, for it is with great humility and a humble hope that this book will generate wider interest and understanding of biathlon in the United States. Novice and dedicated fans alike may appreciate technical details on and athlete accounts of the many elements comprising the sport such as travelling to and navigating around typical venues, physical requirements of training and competing, team and athlete race preparation, rifle construction and marksmanship, ski fabrication and technique, and the diversity of competitions and rules governing the sport, not least of which are efforts to control doping. This 2024 third revision of *Two Skis and a Rifle* (first published late 2017; a minor revision in 2018; 2nd revision mid-2020) includes numerous chapter updates to rules/regulations and other technical details, new and more recent photos and stories from various biathlon events, and a look ahead to 2026 and the XXV Winter Olympic Games in Milano Cortina, Italy.

To appreciate modern biathlon as a world and Olympic sport, we initially must explore the question of why ever did someone slap a pair of skis, or perfectly good pair of wood planks as was the case, to their boots while toting around a rifle in the dead of winter?

Chapter One
From Military Beginnings

Arguably, the sport of biathlon, rather than at one point being the only means of winter travel to hunt and track wild animals, spawned from skiing itself which by one report from evidence of early skis uncovered in areas ranging from Sweden to parts of Asia dates between 6,000-7,000 B.C.[1] Nations located in northern latitudes thereafter, apart from at one point being the only means of winter travel to hunt and track wild animals, effectively utilized skiing in times of civil unrest and for military purposes in territorial border defense. Early reference to militarization of skiing dates to Norwegian civil war and eventual ruler Sverre Sigurdsson and the Birkebeiners in the late 12th and early 13th centuries. Paintings on location at the ski museum in Holmenkollen, Oslo, Norway depict Birkebeiners or Birchlegs as a rebellious faction to the 'pretender' Norse throne Eystein Meyla employing skis and weapons such as bow and arrow, spear, and axe in claiming most of Norway. Upon King Sverre's death in 1202, successor Haakan Sverreson, who died only two years later, left his son Haakon Haakonsson in jeopardy of capture and death from a rival Birkebeiner faction. The Birchlegs, named for using strips of birch tree bark to construct calf high shoes which were strapped to thin wooden skis, took upon themselves the care of young Haakon by ferrying him south from unsettled Osterdalen in Eastern Norway to the safety of Trondheim. Sverreson's heir to the throne later became King Haakan Haakonsson IV who was credited with, among other accomplishments, ending a period of civil unrest and creating the early national and state monarchy in Norway according to European model.[2] King Haakan's journey to safety is remembered annually in the American Birkebeiner ski race held in Hayward, WI, sister event to the Norwegian Birkebeinerrennet.

Image 1.1. Inside the Nordic ski museum at Holmenkollen in Oslo, Norway. (Photo by trabantos/Shutterstock.com)

At about this time, Saxo Grammaticus a notable historian in the late 12th and 13th centuries chronicled early observations of the Danish empire in a series of nine books. Book five, written sometime in the late 1100's or early 1200's, illustrates an encounter between Arngrim, a "champion of Sweden" and the Finns, an "uttermost people of the North". Arngrim in a show of allegiance to King Frode of Danish rule was 'advised' to an 'illustrious service' of fighting King Thengil of Finmark. Riding on curved boards or "skees" the Finns were said to run over ridges that had become impenetrable with snow, but against Angrim's less mobile yet more substantial numbers, they met with little success. In book nine, Grammaticus writes of another encounter

TWO SKIS AND A RIFLE: AN INTRODUCTION TO BIATHLON

between the Finns, led by Prince Matul of Finmark, and Danish King Ragnar whose men were wintering in Permland. With great skill and perhaps revised technique the Finnish archers would glide on "slippery timbers" described as snowskates and approach their enemy at whatever pace desired inflicting damage and then retreating just as quickly as they had approached exhibiting a nimbleness in vehicle and body with "utmost expertness in both advance and flight".[3]

In his pioneering work on the rise of Soviet biathlon, William D. Frank explains early Russian rulers, including Vasily Vasiliyecih Grand Prince of Moscow, had similar interest in using capable skiers to support expansion efforts in the region.[4] One tale purports that Vasily, known as Vasily II 'The Blind', ordered ski militia to drive the ruler of the Golden Horde Mustafa out of what today consists of the Uzbekistan and Kazakhstan regions. Maintaining family ideology, Vasily III 'The Great' subsequently sent ski troops to annex the Tatars, consisting of conquered and reformed groups of Khanates originating from the Golden Horde, out of Siberian regions in the late 1400's. And not to be outdone, Ivan IV 'The Terrible' in the early 1500's sent squads of skiers into Latvia in the lead up to the Livonian War. In perhaps the first mass and cooperative use of ski troops, more than one thousand Russian skiers who along with a regime of Swedish militia led by Russian commander Mikhail Skopin-Shuisky campaigned against the Polish-Lithuanian Commonwealth and successfully relieved the Polish army of the Troitse-Sergievoi Monastery in 1610.[5]

Key players in the regions of Scandinavia and Russia continued to implement ski troops as a means of warfare where bloody battles raged in defense of territory during the Finnish and Napoleonic wars. In the early 1800's, the relationship between the Kingdom of Sweden and Russian Empire devolved as foreign policy imparted by Napoleon and Russian Emperor Alexander I in the Treaty of Trist proved unacceptable to Swedish King Gustav IV Adolf who instead entered into negotiations with Britain. Under threat of Russian invasion, the Swedes, assuming warfare would be unfeasible in the winter, relied on passive border fortification tactics in Finland. Yet Russian ski troops swiftly crossed the border in February overwhelming Swedish resistance which ultimately concluded in the Treaty of Fredrikshamn and subsequent seceding of Swedish Finland to Russia.[5,6] Although skiing with military application began to wane in Norway and Sweden in the early 1800's following the 1814 Treaty of Paris, in the lead up to World War I France, Germany, Austria-Hungary, Italy, and Russia recognized the relevance of ski units for patrol, scouting, and relaying communications.[5,7]

Drawing in the world's greatest economic powers, WWI assembled over nine million combatants on two major sides initially consisting of the Allies with Russia, France and the United Kingdom against the Central Powers of Germany and Austria-Hungary. The assassination of Archduke Franz Ferdinand of Austria triggered a series of events causing expansion of the crisis to involve Italy, Japan and the United States siding with the Allies and the Ottoman Empire and Bulgaria joining the Central Powers.[8,9]

Secret assurances were made in the 1915 Treaty of London which bound Italy to fight within a month of its signing and Italy declared war on Alps bordering Austria-Hungary.[10] Established in 1872, the Alpini military corps of the Italian army originally was commissioned to defend its mountainous borders between Austria and France. That mission changed in WWI as the peacetime Alpini battalions expanded thus beginning a three year campaign in the Alps along the Italian front in the so-called War in Snow and Ice. The Hapsburg War, an early battle of the War in Snow and Ice in 1915, saw regular Alpini alongside specially trained skiing battalions wage siege warfare against Hapsburg

TWO SKIS AND A RIFLE: AN INTRODUCTION TO BIATHLON

(German) mountain troops outfitted with ski infantry of their own. Incidences of ski attacks were limited as high ground positions and heavy artillery on both sides forced troops into the relative safety of snow tunnels excavated in glaciers such as the Marmolada.[11]

Image 1.2. Italian troops advancing on skis along the Alpine front – WWI. (Photo by Igor Golovniov from Corso Battlefield 9-10/1916 "Great War" magazine, Vol. 114, UK/Shutterstock.com)

The collapse of the Russian Empire in WWI left the Grand Duchy of Finland, under Russian monarchy since the early 1800's, in a struggle for national, political, and social power. Political tension between the Russian Czar Nicholas II and the estates of the realm social hierarchy system originating from the Swedish empire divided the Finns into two groups. The 'Reds', led primarily by socialist Democrats, stood opposed to the conservative senate-led ideologies of the 'Whites' to the north. Having been supplied with weaponry from Russia, the Reds waged an unsuccessful offensive in early 1918 having been countered by the German reinforced Whites. The Whites emerged victorious after several milestone battles yet the decimated Reds were reluctant to surrender and thus began a period of political terror. In the wake of the conflicts the Finns traded hands from a Russian to proposed German/Finnish monarchy, but the defeat of the Germans in WWI gave Finland a window of opportunity for its senate to establish independence in 1917 and sovereignty in 1918.[12] The period that followed Finland's independence saw tensions escalate over control of the Karilean Isthmus on the border of Finland and the Soviet Union.

On 30th November 1939, Soviet forces invaded Finland advancing north-east towards the village of Suomussalmi in the contemporary region of Kainuu with the objective of dividing Finland in half at the city of Oulu. With troops approaching 14,000 men from two rifle divisions, Soviets, maneuvering heavy artillery, tanks, and trucks, advancing along Raate Road were met with swift and agile Finnish ski troops that splintered the Soviets into smaller disorganized groups in a tactic known as 'motti'.[13] The result was a near complete annihilation of the Soviets and capture of military supplies and a morale boost for the Finns following what arguably was the single most impressive ski warfare incursion in history.

Finland initially continued their belligerence against the Soviets by joining the Axis powers of Germany, Italy, and Japan who were fighting against the Allies of the Soviet Union, United States, and much of Europe during World War II. In what has come to be known as the Great Patriotic War, the two main protagonists, Nazi Germany and opposing Soviet Union, remained disillusioned over territorial loss in the aftermath of WWI. Hitler had declared his intent to invade Russia on 11th August 1939 citing that the Soviet annexations of Baltic and Romanian territories were in violation of the non-aggression Molotov-Ribbentrop Pact. For nearly two years the Soviet border was quiet as Germany preoccupied themselves with conquering parts of Scandinavia and France until German and Axis forces crossed the border on 22nd June, 1941 in the summertime Operation Barbarossa offensive. While advancing on Moscow, Hitler, in a decision with severe ramifications, overruled field commanders' strategies and delayed progressing on the capital city citing the importance of capturing Soviet industrial, mining, and agricultural resources. Autumn 1941 saw German panzer groups and Heer Wehrmacht divisions advance to within 30km of Moscow but exhaustion and the onset of freezing temperatures in December suspended further attacks to reach the Kremlin.[14] Under Marshal Shaposhnikov the Soviets led a counter-offensive against the Germans along an eighty kilometer front employing winter guerrilla tactics learned from the Finns. With the intent of blocking a German supply line to the front, Soviet paratroopers along with five ski battalions led an attack against the elite Wehrmacht near Moscow.[4] It became clear after gaining several hundred kilometers in some sectors of the battle that the Russians had learned considerably from the Winter War against Finland by effectively using ski troops on a massive scale.[15]

Earlier in the War, the Germans in 1940 had advanced on Norway and laid siege to the Vemork hydroelectric plant with intentions of using heavy water, a byproduct of fertilizer production at the plant, to manufacture nuclear weapons. The German Uranverein nuclear weapon program, likened to the Manhattan project in the United States, took shape in early 1939 after nuclear fission had been discovered months earlier by Otto Hahn and Fritz Strassmann. The Germans understood that heavy water served as an effective medium in nuclear reactor design and was needed to generate the necessary fissile material plutonium for constructing a nuclear bomb. Intelligence secured in 1941 by Allied nations provided a detailed risk assessment of Vemork's role in Uranverein which in 1942 led to their planning of elaborate saboteur operations to destroy the plant since bombing raids had high potential for civilian casualties. Operations Grouse and

Gunnerside commenced with two teams of Norwegian paratroopers, rendezvousing on the snowy Hardanger-Vidda region of Norway, steadily making their way on skis to the mountainous territory around Vemork. Final preparations were made by the combined team in late February 1943 and a plan was developed to covertly mine the heavy water electrolysis chambers in the plant.[16] The mission went virtually without a hitch and was considered a great success as the hero saboteurs skied to safety in a tale chronicled in several books and popularized in the 1965 film 'Heroes of Telemark' starring Kirk Douglas.

Image 1.3. Vemork heavy water hydroelectric plant and surrounding mountainous terrain. (Photo by Scandphoto/Shutterstock.com)

As unlikely as it may seem, in 1941 Australian Commonwealth troops worked closely with British Allied forces to wage a campaign against Vichy French forces in the snow-covered mountains in Lebanon

(Cedars), Syria. Many of the Australian troops had never seen snow and independently took to skiing for the first time while the country's army more formally created the 9th Division Ski Battalion, training its soldiers in the art of ski warfare in case the Germans decided to push farther south.[17] Elsewhere, the United States caught wind of the success that Finnish ski troops had over Russia in the Winter War of 1939 and Charles Minot Dole, president of the National Ski Patrol at the time, lobbied for a similarly trained unit in mountain warfare for the U.S. Army. Out of the 10 divisions originally planned, the 10th Mountain Division would become the only active duty regimen under the eventual command of Major General George Price Hays in 1944.[18] Equipped with winter weather gear, white camouflage, and skis, the division trained in the craft of mountain warfare in preparation for deployment in Italy. The late winter of 1944/1945 saw the division along with army infantry successfully enter into combat with the Germans in the northern Apennines Mountains liberating Po Valley for the advancing Allies.[19] In recognition of their success, some thirty members of the original 10th Mountain Division were inducted into the United States Ski Hall of Fame with dozens congregating at the 2006 Hannes Schneider Meister Cup Race event in New Hampshire.[20]

Many nations continue to train troops in ski and mountain warfare to this day including the United States at the Marine Corps Mountain Warfare Training Center in northern California, the Northern Warfare Training Center and Naval Special Warfare Cold Weather Detachment in Alaska, and the Army Mountain Warfare School in central Vermont. Yet in this modern peacetime era for most mountain/ski special forces, there remains one conflict of notable interest; the Siachen War between India and Pakistan over the glacier region in Kashmir. The UN-mediated Karachi Agreement of 1949 left an area of undemarcated territory about one thousand square miles in the

Karakoram range, home to such important mountaineering destinations as yet unclimbed Saltoro Kangri II (7,705 meters). In 1984, India led a successful offensive in Operation Meghdoot claiming control of much of the glacier and major passes in the region while Pakistan was left with lower glacial valleys. After Meghdoot, several major combat operations on both sides have occurred as recently as the 2003 ceasefire with Pakistan intent on reclaiming lost territory. Nearly one hundred fifty manned outposts with some three thousand mountain/ski warfare trained troops remain along an 'actual ground position line' in Kashmir while India, in a show of defiant control over Pakistan, has as recently as 2007 continued to allow mountaineering expeditions to climb the higher peaks of the Siachen glacier.[21] Training for such conflicts even if troops never saw military action would lie at the heart of friendly competitions between nations and would lead to the rise of biathlon as a sporting pastime.

Chapter Two
To the Sport of Biathlon

Biathlon was first observed in the Olympics in 1960 and prior to being simply a feat from the Greek for "two tests or events", the sport arguably spawned from the contemporary pentathlon competition devised by Baron Pierre de Coubertin, founder of the modern Olympic Games.[1] As a successor to the original pentathlon of the ancient Olympic games, modern pentathlon similarly has athletes competing in five events originally held over five days from 1912-1980 and now on one day in its current format. Coubertin believed that pentathlon would test "a man's moral qualities as much as his physical resources and skills, producing thereby a complete athlete."[2] Pentathletes receive performance-based points for each competition which consists of single touch round robin fencing followed by a 200 meter freestyle swim. After a change of clothing, athletes are faced with a show jumping competition on unfamiliar horses randomly assigned by the Union Internationale de Pentathlon Moderne (UIPM), the governing body of modern pentathlon. The finale combines two events and is quite similar conceptually to winter biathlon where pentathletes, using a laser pistol which in 2014 replaced air pistols, must stop and hit a target five times repeated on four separate occasions while concurrently running a total distance of 3,200 meters or just under two miles. The person who amasses the most points in the first three events sets off on the combined laser-run first with the remaining athletes starting after a time penalty based on their point differential thus ensuring the winner across the line is the true gold medal recipient.[3]

Modern pentathletes during World War II solicited the International Olympic Committee (IOC) to establish a winter pentathlon competition to be held at the Winter Olympic Games. Instead of the swimming and running competitions of summer pentathlon, athletes would need to excel in snow disciplines including 12 kilometer (km) cross-country and 3 km downhill skiing events according to International Ski Federation (FIS) rules. Carry overs from summer pentathlon would include shooting, fencing, and horse riding yet after an informal trial run of the competition in 1942 winter pentathlon would only be included once as a demonstration sport at the 1948 St. Moritz Olympic Games under the direction of Major Willy Grundbacher.[1,4] Sweden's Gustaf Lindh would become the first and only winner of the event while second place finisher, Willie Grut, also Swedish, placed second and would later that year go on to win gold in modern pentathlon at the 1948 London summer Olympic Games.[5] Winter pentathlon apparently received little universal interest both from global participatory (only five nations competed in winter pentathlon) and IOC perspectives and was never included at the Olympics again. Yet the idea of a multi-discipline event at the Winter Olympics remained on the minds of certain UIPM and IOC organizers and perhaps they should have looked no further than the 'military patrol' competition, which had been a part of the official Olympic program since 1924.

As early as 1767, ski and shooting competitions along the Norwegian and Swedish border occurred as a means of military training and in 1861 the Tyrsil Rifle and Ski Club in Norway enrolled fifty-two members and is often considered the oldest club of its kind. As a physical test for nations with special mountain military units, athletes competed in team military patrol events incorporating cross-country skiing, mountaineering, and rifle shooting. Military patrol followed a similar premise as today's biathlon but was longer encompassing 25 km (15 km for women) of skiing, albeit with four-member patrol teams, and target shooting using a small bore rifle carried along with a backpack. Patrols were required to climb over the duration of the course between 500 to 1,200 meters (300 to 700 meters for women) and teams consisted of one officer and non-officer alike along with two privates. When originally conceived, the officer carried a pistol instead of a rifle and did not take part in shooting and instead other members of the patrol carried rifles and a 24 kilogram (kg) backpack shooting targets at a distance of 250 meters. Each member of the patrol, minus the officer, would take six shots at the target hitting as many as possible with thirty second time bonuses on offer for each hit. The first official military patrol competition happened in Germany in 1902 and subsequently the race made its way into the Nordic Games (Nordiska Spelen) winter sports contests of 1922.[6] In its inaugural race at the 1924 winter Olympics in Chamonix, France, a team of swift skiing Swiss athletes led by Denis Vaucher hit eight targets and won gold over Finland and France in a time of 3:56:06.[7] Thereafter, military patrol, along with winter pentathlon's sole inclusion in 1948, was relegated to demonstration sport status, following growing anti-military public opinion, with teams from Norway winning at St. Moritz in 1928,[8] Italy in 1936 at Garmisch-Partenkirchen,[9] and finally Switzerland again at St. Moritz in 1948.[4]

Military patrol's foundation of friendly competition in times around World War II drew wider global appreciation and launched sister events such as the Patrouille des Glaciers (PDG) ski mountaineering race held now every two years in Switzerland. Initiated in 1943 by two Swiss captains in the 10th Mountain Brigade, the aim of competition was for three-member troops to demonstrate operational readiness by traversing a course running from Zermatt to Verbier, otherwise known as the Haute Route. The first two editions were well received, but tragedy struck during the third race in 1949 when a Swiss team on their way from Arolla to Verbier fell to their deaths on the glaciated terrain of Monte Mine forcing the Federal Military Department to cancel further races. Yet the lore of the race lived on and in 1983 Chief of Swiss Armed Forces Training Lieutenant General Roger Mabillard authorized the reintroduction of the PDG. Today the PDG has witnessed immense growth attracting thousands of military and civilian competitors from many nations and for the first time in 2004, a foreign team won the race. Such popularity has raised concern in the media over athletes using performance enhancing drugs (PED) and for a time the PDG was run under an athlete self-governed 'spirit of competition' clause; however, all registered athletes are now subject to doping control.[10] Modern biathlon itself has not been immune to controversy over PED use upon release of the McLaren Report in 2016 (see Chapter Seven), but despite such moral dilemmas facing sport, biathlon has not lost favor in the public eye.

…

The UIPM in 1948 began lobbying the IOC in earnest for the inclusion of winter pentathlon in the Olympics; however, the logistics of running five events proved insurmountable as few venues could physically host such a competition in the aftermath of World War II. In the years that followed, the UIPM under the direction of Sven Thofelt (SWE) along with seventeen nations, with input from the IOC itself indicating a preference to narrow the focus to cross-country skiing and rifle shooting, renamed modern pentathlon to biathlon. Biathlon soon became recognized as an international sport by the IOC with the advent of competition rules ratified in 1956 and being officially governed by the UIPM in 1957 (later to become the International Union of Modern Pentathlon and Biathlon or UIPMB in 1967). In 1958, the UIPM proposed an inaugural world championships to be held in Saalfelden, Austria showcasing individual and team events and would ultimately be dominated by Sweden. At the 55th session of the

TWO SKIS AND A RIFLE: AN INTRODUCTION TO BIATHLON

IOC held from 25th-29th May 1959 in Munich, Germany, UIPM President Gustaf Dryssen pleaded with IOC committee members for biathlon to be included in the Winter Olympic Games.[11,12] Dryssen's request was favorably received and future inclusion of biathlon on the official program would be contingent on its success at the 1960 Olympic Games in Squaw Valley, CA.[13]

Early versions of biathlon under the auspices of the UIPM looked vastly different than today. Beginning with the inaugural World Championships in 1958, biathletes, starting at two minute intervals, would ski a 20 km course while periodically stopping to take five shots at a target using a large bore rifle in the prone (or lying flat on the stomach) position at distances of 250, 200, and 150 meters and once in the standing position at a distance of 100 meters. Targets were made of cardboard measuring 30, 25, 20 and 30 centimeters (cm), respectively, to coincide with the shooting position and distance and should a competitor miss a shot, two minutes would be added to his aggregate time. However, to facilitate organization of the event and in the safety interests of spectators and competitors alike, the UIPM dropped this 'old program' and adopted in 1965 a format that appears very similar to today where biathletes ski around designated loops stopping and resuming each lap at a single shooting range.[6,11,14] Alternating between prone and standing positions, biathletes would ski into the range and take aim at paper targets measuring 250 millimeters (mm) with a bullseye of 125 mm for prone and 500 mm (350 mm bullseye) for standing positions. After officials had analyzed the targets, missing the main target or the bullseye in either position would result in time penalties of one and two minutes, respectively.[15] Use of paper targets had several drawbacks, not least of which was a lack of instantaneous feedback for both athletes and spectators. Conceivably biathletes would only learn their fate and final race position after officials had examined paper targets and the race had been long concluded.

Two years later in 1960 biathlon would debut at the Winter Olympic Games at Squaw Valley, CA with the men's 20 km competition. Captain Rolf Gerlofson, UIPM appointed technical delegate, was charged with finding a suitable location for the event as early as 1957 and construction of shooting ranges with final refinements were completed in summer 1959. Four firing ranges with 'pull-type' targets located at varying distances were placed strategically around a course shared with other cross-country skiing events at 6.5 km for the 200 meter range, 9.5 km - 250 meter range, 12.5 km – 150 meter range, and 15 km – 100 meter range. In the final report of the games[16], transitioning from paper targets proved challenging.

> Since there was no record of pull targets being used in previous biathlon competition, it was necessary to design and construct a system. A simple 'sleeve and plunger' system was devised, enabling Chief of Race Birger Torrissen and his crews to raise and lower targets when changing them. Thus, the target could be changed and the results relayed to the scorekeeper immediately after each competitor completed his five rounds of shooting. (118)

Held at the McKinney Creek Stadium in Tahoma on 21st February, 1960, Sweden's Klas Ivar Vilhelm Lestander placed 15th in skiing but won gold after 'cleaning' or hitting all twenty targets, besting the field after a feat never before seen in international competition. Results from each shooting range were phoned to the stadium area, announced to spectators, and posted on a scoreboard. Nine nations with thirty athletes in total entered the inaugural event under the supervision of an officer from the United States Air Force Rifle School and the success of biathlon at Squaw Valley solidified its future in the Winter Olympic Games.[16]

Image 2.1. American Sean Doherty competing in the men's 20 km individual race at the Pokljuka, Slovenia World Cup on December 6, 2018. (Photo by Julia_Sadykova/Shutterstock.com)

Until 1964 at the Winter Olympics and 1966 at the World Championships the sole event was the men's individual 20 km race, although the concept of a team competition was on the mind of organizers from the beginning. Early team events used the individual race times of the top three biathletes from each nation to produce an overall team time and the national team with the lowest aggregate time was declared the winner. First held unofficially in 1965, the first official team event was held in 1966 at the Garmisch-Partenkirchen World Championships and followed a 4 x 7.5 km format where four biathletes, initially with one member from each nation starting en masse, would one after another ski a 7.5 km course. Including the inaugural men's 4 x 7.5 km relay event at the 1968 Grenoble-Autrans Winter Olympics, a team from the Soviet Union would in a show of early dominance win Olympic gold no fewer than six times running until Germany finally broke the Soviet win streak in 1992.[17]

Biathlon targets would evolve from the initial paper medium to breakable balloons or glass (still a far cry from today's electro-mechanically controlled metal targets; see chapter six) and each team member would carry sixteen rounds of ammunition hand loading individual penalty rounds after a missed shot.[11] Due to the high cost of ammunition and loud discharge noise, safety concerns, and difficulty obtaining gun licenses, the UIPMB began to explore smaller bore rifles at the 1972 World Junior Biathlon Championships. Lessons learned from that event eventually led to a proposal that was approved at the 1976 Biathlon Congress in Seefeld, Austria to officially introduce the small bore .22 caliber rifle. The 1977 Vingrom, Norway World Championships marked the last time that large bore rifles would be used in competition and on January 1st, 1978 the transition to a .22 LR (long rifle), which is still in use today, dramatically transformed the sport of biathlon.[15,18]

The sport continued to mature growing in stature in the late 1970's with the advent of the first World Cup event on 13th January, 1978. Using a slightly modified system than at present (see Chapter Three), biathletes competed over a season long competition in three disciplines (20 km individual, 10 km sprint, and 4 x 7.5 km team relay) with points on offer for individual and team placings. The first of four events was held in Ruhpolding, Germany with the finale in Sodankyla, Finland and was dominated by German and Russian biathletes who between them took the top seven final season ending placings. Frank Ullrich from Germany will be remembered as the first World Cup champion

TWO SKIS AND A RIFLE: AN INTRODUCTION TO BIATHLON

and remained actively involved in the sport as a trainer for the German national team.[19]

...

The world would have to wait until 1981 for the first women's international biathlon competition held at Jachymov-Karlovy Vary in the current Czech Republic. The UIPMB would continue to elevate the status of women's competition and in 1982-83 created a season long competition based on the men's World Cup model. Called the European Championships, even though competition was not restricted to European nations per se, three venues were originally scheduled beginning with a return to Jachymov; however, that and another race in Oberhof, Germany were canceled leaving Lappeenranta, Finland as the only race held that season. Dominated by Norwegian and Finnish biathletes, Gry Ostvik from Norway became the first female overall World Cup winner. Women's biathlon over the next decade continued to see tremendous growth with inclusion of 10 km and 5 km individual and 3 x 5 km team races at the 1984 World Championships and formation of a joint men's and women's (no longer a European Cup) World Cup held over the 1987-88 season.[20] Such a rise in women's biathlon participation at the international level would eventually culminate at the 1992 Winter Olympic Games in Albertville, France at the Les Saisies cross-country skiing and biathlon venue. Held on 11th February, 1992, the now longer 7.5 km sprint competition would be the first ever Olympic event for women where biathletes stopped twice to shoot five times, first in the prone position at 2.5 km and again at 5 km for the standing position, before racing the final 2.5 km to the finish. Anfisa Rezstova of Russia, competing under the Unified Team Olympic rings flag, won inaugural gold in a time of 24:29.2 having missed three shots along the way. The women's 15 km (won by Antje Misersky of Germany) and 3 x 7.5 km relay (presently a 4 x 6 km competition; won by France) events would also make their Olympic debut at Albertville. In total, twenty-seven nations sent biathletes to compete in the XVI Olympic Winter Games, six more than the previous edition held at the Canmore Nordic Center in Alberta, Canada.[17,21]

Image 2.2. Early action during the women's 4 x 6 km relay race from the 2019 Hochfilzen, Austria World Cup with Karoline Offigstad Knotten of team Norway leading the way. (Photo by Pierre Teyssot/Shutterstock.com)

Later that same year citing global growth and interest in the sport as well as a rationale proposed by UIPMB, a decision was made to separate biathlon from modern pentathlon on November 30th, 1992 in Amelie-Les-Bains, France, compelling biathlon to form its own federation. An agreement was made at an extraordinary congress of the

TWO SKIS AND A RIFLE: AN INTRODUCTION TO BIATHLON

UIPMB in London on July 2nd, 1993 to retain UIPMB as the umbrella organization and allow the UIPM and newly named International Biathlon Union (IBU) to operate autonomously. However, the IOC did not recognize IBU as an official federation until August 20th, 1998 after several acts of effective self-governance had transpired in the intervening years including internal IBU Congresses and oversight of international competitions. Later that year the Global Association of International Sports Federations (GAISF) granted IBU official status registering its seat as an international federation on June 1st, 1999 in Salzburg, Austria and from this momentous point in time, the IBU has remained the sport's governing body. Along the way and usually after trial runs at IBU (see chapter 4) or World Cup venues, new events would find their way into the World Championships (WC) and Olympics (O) including the mass start (WC - 1999; O - 2006), pursuit (WC - 1997; O - 2002 men, 2006 women), mixed relay (WC – 2005; O - 2014), and single mixed relay (WC – 2019) competitions. Since 2014 the Olympics hosts six biathlon events (eleven races in total) for both men and women (individual, relay, sprint, pursuit, mass start, and mixed relay).[20,22,23] New additions to the calendar include the men's and women's super sprint (with both a qualifying and final race) which debuted at the Oslo, Norway 2021 World Cup event, and the short individual race held during the Italian World Cup in 2024.[22,24] Perhaps these exciting new competitions, essentially shorter versions of their respective full distance races, which the IBU continues to promote may too may find their way onto the World Championship and Olympic programs. See table 2.1 below for an illustration of the current races on offer by the IBU at venues such as the World Championships and Olympic Winter Games.[25]

Table 2.1. List of IBU Biathlon Competition Formats and Inclusion at Noteworthy Events

Competition Format	World Championships[4]	Olympics[5]
Individual (M + W)	✓	✓
Short Individual (M + W)[1]	X	X
Mass Start 30 (M + W)	✓	✓
Mass Start 60 (M + W)[2]	X	X
Pursuit (M + W)	✓	✓
Sprint (M + W)	✓	✓
Relay (M + W)	✓	✓
Mixed Relay 2.0 km loop	✓	✓
Single Mixed Relay men or women first	✓	X
Super Sprint Qualification (M + W)[3]	X	X
Super Sprint Final (M + W)[3]	X	X

Notes: ✓ = currently on program; X = not currently on program; [1] = first held at the German IBU Cup in 2019 and Italian World Cup in 2024; [2] = first held at the Martell-Val Martello (Italy) IBU Cup in 2019; [3] = first held at the Khanty-Mansiysk (Russia) IBU Cup in 2018 and Norwegian World Cup in 2021; [4] = current through the 2024 World Championships; [5] = current through the 2026 Winter Olympic Games.

Chapter Three
Venues and Events

The World Cup circuit, at the highest level known as the BMW IBU World Cup, traditionally begins in November or December where snow has already fallen in northern Scandinavian climates and follows a primarily ten event European schedule. Competitions at each venue occur over several days, giving athletes sufficient time to recover between various races such as the sprint, mass start, pursuit, and relay events. While the IBU attempts to minimize travel between competitions through a program of traditional hosts that enjoy a deep fan base and modern facilities, several up-and-coming venues such as Annecy-Le Grand Bornard (FRA; a regular stop since the 2017/2018 season), Lenzerheide (SWI; host of the 2024 World Championships), and Otepaa (EST; on the schedule for 2026) are consistently making their way onto the rotation of World Cup events. Yet it is at these long-standing venues, such as the 2023 World Championships in Oberhof, Germany that witnessed some 150,000 fans cheer on their favorite biathletes, where the sport has solidified its global appeal.

Ostersund, Sweden and the Single and Team Mixed Relay Races

The city of Ostersund, Sweden, part of the Jamtland province and located along the shores of Lake Storjson, has hosted World Cup level biathlon on numerous occasions and is considered the cultural and economic center in the region. With a total population of almost 50,000, Ostersund is the largest city in northern Sweden and home of Mid Sweden University's largest campus to some 7,000 students. At a latitude over 63° north, the city has a subarctic climate but receives cold arctic winds called Nordvastan or Kallvastan depending on their direction of origin. However, the winter climate in Ostersund is more temperate than other locales at similar high latitude due to the currents of the Atlantic Gulf Stream which bring warmer breezes and an average November daily mean temperature of -0.5°C (31°F). Low average monthly precipitation levels of less than two inches necessitates creativity to ensure there is sufficient snow cover to once again have Ostersund play an early host for the next several World Cup seasons.[1]

In today's fickle climate, early season more often than not means a lack of snow for winter events such as cross-country skiing which are often held at lower altitudes near the flatter base of mountainous terrain. Along with traditional alpinesque snowmaking machines, for several years dating back to 2001 organizers of major winter events, including the 2014 Winter Olympics in Sochi, have experimented with storing or 'farming' millions of cubic feet of snow from the previous winter to help fill in gaps or even completely cover areas of a cross-country ski course the following early winter season. Essentially snow is stockpiled and covered over the duration of the spring and summer months with natural or fabricated insulating materials such as wood chips, saw dust, plastic sheets, or thermal foam. For recent biathlon seasons, the Ostersund Municipality stored two snow piles each totaling 30,000 cubic meters (one cubic meter is roughly the volume of a typical washer and dryer) under 40 cm (15 inches) of sawdust, trucking as many as 400 loads to the biathlon stadium.[2] In what must feel like opening an early Christmas present, the insulating material is removed to uncover last year's snow which, although not the best quality, serves its purpose to add base to any natural or artificial (man-made) snow along the skiing course.

With COVID-19 restrictions in the rear-view mirror, a festival like atmosphere kicked off the 2023/2024 World Cup season at the Swedish national biathlon stadium located two kilometers from the city center of Ostersund, a casual walk for many a spectator. Accordingly, all biathlon venues include a start/finish area, shooting range and penalty loop located very close to one another, a relay hand-over zone, and spectator areas including a grandstand and roped areas around the skiing course. Numerous technical areas abound near the stadium including a very private team waxing hut, athlete and team lounge and changing rooms, and commentator boxes to broadcast live streaming and radio shows around the globe. Teams are often housed very close to the venue either on premises or in the nearby city to ease travel for on-course practice and warming-up prior to competition.[3]

The World Cup season racing at Ostersund began by highlighting the mixed and single mixed relay events on November 25th, 2023, now becoming more and more popular on the World Cup competition calendar. Just as with all other races, the course for the relay events must meet strict requirements and not exceed an altitude of 1,800 meters above sea level and be held on a six meter wide groomed snow surface with additional space at the outskirts for coaching and television crews. On steeper uphill terrain which may be as significant as 25% gradient (1 foot increase in elevation for every 4 feet of flat/horizontal skiing), the course is widened to allow ease of passing where overall fitness and stamina are more important than drafting at other faster points on the course. For both mixed relay events, each national federation (e.g., United States Biathlon) fields a team of biathletes and in the case of the single mixed relay one male and one female competitor, and for the mixed team event, two of each gender.[4]

The first competitor from each nation, wearing a red bib and starting in position based on the Nations Cup score (a separate competition which combines scores for each nation's top women and men biathletes) determined by the previous top three biathletes' results from each nation, set off as a group according to sex over a 1.5 or 2 km loop shooting at least once (twice in the single mixed event) in both the prone and standing positions. Unique mostly to the relay events, if a biathlete fails to hit one of the five targets during each shooting, they are allowed to individually load up to three more bullets to try and hit any remaining missed targets. Beyond those three extra rounds of ammunition, should any targets remain missed, the biathlete must ski away from the range as normal and enter a 150 meter (75 meter for single mixed events) penalty loop sector rather than continuing on course. The advantage certainly belongs to teams that hit all targets as extra time is needed to both load new bullets and ski the penalty loop.[4]

In these exciting competitions where national pride boils over in the stadium, nations alternate between men and women competitors skiing over predetermined distances with a pattern of shooting common to the relay events. Once a leg is finished, biathletes ski into a well-marked hand-over zone that is thirty meters long and nine meters wide. Subsequent starts by each respective national team member, now wearing a green bib (with yellow and blue to follow as necessary depending on the event), occur once the incoming skier tags on the shoulder or other part of the body the outgoing biathlete in the hand over zone, which is watched closely and confirmed with an arm gesture by IBU officials. In the single mixed relay event, either women or men may start first depending on the rules of the day and ski over a 1.5 km loop. Following each loop, a biathlete will shoot first in the prone and then standing position and then ski a short distance to tag their fellow compatriot; a scenario repeated twice in total by each nation's competitor. Whoever starts second, however, is considered the anchor leg for the competition since instead of tagging in a teammate at the last shoot, a final ski over the 1.5 km loop is required to reach the finish line. As such, the first skier off during the single mixed relay skis a total distance of 6 km while the second biathlete skis an extra 1.5 km or 7.5 km in total. The mixed relay follows a similar format although there are four members per national team (two women and men each) with each teammate shooting twice (once each in the prone and standing positions) and skiing a total of 6 km if women start first and 7.5 km if the men lead off in a 3 x 2 km or 3 x 2.5 km format, respectively.[4] Serendipitously enough, a team from Sweden, at their home stadium, and also France took top honors in the single mixed and mixed relay events at Ostersund in 2023, respectively. As a highlight for the United States, Susan Dunklee and Sean Doherty impressively took bronze at the final single mixed relay race of the 2020/2021 season in Nove Mesto Na Morave (CZE).[5]

Pokljuka, Slovenia and the Sprint Race

A fixture on the race calendar, Pokljuka, Slovenia has been a regular World Cup stop for many years and even hosted the World Championships in 2021. The biathlon center is located on a flat and forested karst plateau situated at approximately 1,345 meters elevation in the Triglav National Park of northwestern Slovenia. The closest village of any significance is Bled about 15 km to the west and is where virtually everyone stays, if not traveling separately in a personal RV, including the top 25 best ranked male and female athletes (top 30 for the World Championships) who receive free accommodations according to the financial responsibilities of the IBU. During the 2016/2017 season, the World Cup traveled initially from Pokljuka approximately 2,400 km due south to Ostersund presenting teams with a logistical nightmare of transporting athletes, coaches, skis, and rifles across an international border.[6]

The Pokljuka and Ostersund organizing committees, just as with other host venues, undertake much of the leg work to ease travel to a region by preparing charter flights and transportation to and from the closest major airport or train station. Team vehicles making a border crossing must present a valid weapon possession license secured from their country of origin, declare radio devices that may not be coordinated/approved, and prove medicinal needs for all prescription drugs. Personnel driving cars and vans may also be required to secure toll stickers or vignettes in certain countries to use motorways or run the risk of severe fines. Athletes and teams are further required to maintain valid accident and health insurance and have visas secured prior to entering a country. In the case of Pokljuka, the organizing committee provides free of charge transportation from Bled to the biathlon arena on a regular basis. As teams travel from one venue to another, they are presented with the same, albeit nuanced per the country in question, logistical challenges and fortunately, many World Cup venue organizing committees have chiefs of accommodation, travel, and accreditation to aid in the process.[7] In the end, it is imperative that athletes be sheltered from the headaches of travel to limit distress and maximize rest, preparation, and readiness for competition.

A highlight of any World Cup venue are the women's and men's sprint races which, as the name implies, involve brief high intensity efforts over shorter distances with less frequent stops at the shooting range. At most World Cup events, the starting list of athletes is spread over four groups or 'draws'. Captains or coaches from each team select in which draw each top competitor will be placed and then a random selection by IBU determines the starting order within each draw. This offers several strategic advantages and challenges for coaches who seek to place their top athletes in the best draw possible. Changing weather conditions, deterioration of the skiing track, and times and starting positions of other top competitors if known all must be factored into the decision of draw placement, and generally most nations' top competitors are placed in the initial wave. For the sprint competition, athletes normally start one after another at thirty second intervals by passing through a retractable gate at the starting line. A nearby timing clock counts down remaining seconds to everyone's start time and emits an audible beep giving the cue to go. Care is taken to start as close to the beep as possible; however, athletes are given +/- 3 seconds to activate the gate and their official start time for the sprint race.[4]

Image 3.1. Tarjei Boe, older brother to Johannes Thignes Boe, in action and on his way to a 4th place finish in the sprint race during the Pokljuka, Slovenia World Cup on December 7, 2018. (Photo by Julia_Sadykova/Shutterstock.com)

Once on course, the men ski around 3.3 km loops for a total of 10 km and stop to shoot once after each loop in the prone and standing positions (ski/P/ski/S/ski). Women follow a similar pattern; however, skiing is held over a shorter 7.5 km distance involving three 2.5 km loops. For the sprint and other competitions, a penalty loop is situated approximately sixty meters immediately after the shooting range. The loop itself is a familiar six meters wide and 150 meters long that, should a biathlete miss any number of the five requisite targets, adds approximately 20-25 seconds of ski time per miss. Perfect shooting is priority one in the sprint race which is often decided by a handful of seconds and Norway's reigning star Johannes Thignes Boe and Sweden's Elvira Oeberg both shot and skied the fastest times in their respective races at the 2023 Pokljuka World Cup.

Nove Mesto, Czech Republic and the Mass Start Race

Perhaps no other stop on the World Cup circuit garners as much fanfare as the Vysocina Biathlon Arena in Nove Mesto, Czech Republic. Located in a mountainous region and home locally to some 10,500 people, the Nove Mesto Na More (NMNM) biathlon stadium swells to capacity seeing some 30,000 fans flocking to daily events while one in ten Czechs watch competition unfold live on European television. Daily stadium tickets sell out fast and cost anywhere from 10-20 dollars and fans traveling from distant locales are encouraged to buy tickets early as more than 120,000 spectators watch the races unfold in person over four days. Such a fan base in the Czech Republic and at other venues is not unheard of since biathlon remains the most widely viewed sport during the European winter months.[8]

The stadium area becomes a festival of sounds, sights, and smells with fans cheering for whatever they like needing no reason at all. Some have even started or are members of fan clubs and bring banners in display of their favorite national hero like Arnd Pfeiffer from Germany or Norway's Johannes Thignes Boe. At the race start and finish, the host commentator rouses the crowd and plays American music such as Bruce Springsteen, Bon Jovi, and Queen over the loudspeaker while urging competitors to the finish line as fans frenziedly cheer and wave their national flags. Although rules prohibit extravagantly loud devices such as air horns in the arena, cow bells, horns, whistles, and swirling rasp sound makers create a symphony of music unique to biathlon. When a national hero like the Czech Republic's very own Marketa Davidova enters the shooting range, the stadium crowd lulls into a hush where anything more than a whisper becomes a distraction. Noisemakers are silenced as spectators hang on every shot letting out an audible and very brief "yeah!" with each hit target only to be followed by an "aww!" after the unfortunate miss.

The mass start race brings its own level of excitement as each nations' top athletes simultaneously start on a grid formatted similarly to running races with the fastest athletes at front. Starting positions are predetermined by an athlete's total World Cup score (accumulated points to date; see Chapter Four) with the top 25 ranked athletes, along with 5 athletes performing particularly well at the time, lined up at front and noted along the sides of the starting area using colored nylon marker boards placed in the snow. After a brief wait and countdown from 1.5 minutes, an official fires a start pistol and, similar to track events, if a biathlete starts too early an official will sound the pistol once more for a restart. Each athlete skis five loops for a total of 15 km and 12.5 km for men and women (3 km loops for men and 2.5 km loops for women), respectively, shooting periodically in the prone and standing positions (ski/P/ski/P/ski/S/ski/S/ski) with misses subjecting the racer to a penalty loop(s).[4] Both the women's and men's mass start events went smoothly and in what seemingly had a fairy tale ending on December 18th, 2016, the Czech Republic's very own Gabriella Koukalova missed only one shot on her way to crossing the finish line alone in first just 3.1 seconds in front of Laura Dahlmeier (GER) to the delight of a roaring home crowd.

Image 3.2. Nove Mesto Na More Vysocina biathlon arena playing host to the 2013 IBU World Championships. (Photo by Patrik Mezirka/Shutterstock.com)

Oberhof and Ruhpolding, Germany and the Pursuit Race

The transient circus that is the biathlon World Cup consistently work their way to Germany for two stops, Oberhof and Ruhpolding. Separated themselves by 640 km and each hosting World Cups for the foreseeable future, Oberhof and Ruhpolding are winter sports meccas with well-established biathlon arenas. The DKB ski arena in Oberhof is located two kilometers from the center of town sitting at 814 meters altitude with sufficient room to host over 10,000 spectators. Like Ostersund and several other arenas, Oberhof has significant snow farming and generating capabilities guaranteeing sufficient snow cover during difficult weather conditions.[9] The Chiemgau arena in Ruhpolding is even larger with capacity for 23,000 spectators including

13,000 in the stands and room for an additional 10,000 along the course, which depending on course loop length could well be worth the hike to be only a few feet away from the finest biathletes in the world.[10]

The 12.5 km and 10 km pursuit events for men and women, respectively, have been a part of major biathlon competition since the 1997 World Championships in Brezno-Orsblie, Slovakia, and are held at most World Cup events. Unlike most other biathlon races that have group/mass or consecutive individually timed starts, the pursuit uses the finishing times from a qualifying race, usually a sprint race or less commonly a mass start or individual event held prior at the same venue, to determine pursuit (an apropos name when the goal is to chase down and pass biathletes starting beforehand) starting times for all biathletes. Competitors in the pursuit start in the same order as they finished the qualifying race with the winner being granted start number one, the second place finisher with bib two, and so on. The winner of the qualifying race is given a start time of zero (0 min: 0 sec) and all remaining competitors begin afterwards in one of four starting chutes based on their own individual time behind the winner of the qualifying race. For example, Frenchman Martin Fourcade won the 2020 Ruhpolding men's sprint competition in a time of 22:41:05 followed by second place finisher and compatriot Quentin Fillon Maillet (FRA) with a time of 22:44:06, a time difference of just +3.1 seconds. After rounding to the nearest second, Fillon Maillet started his pursuit of Fourcade already on course, after waiting three seconds at the starting line/chute. This same principle is used to send off all remaining competitors in the pursuit race.[5]

Following the same ski/shoot format as the mass start, women and men cover 10 km and 12.5 km by skiing on five occasions 2 km and 2.5 km loops, respectively. One can only imagine the nerves of being first out of the gate with sixty of the world's best biathletes desperately trying to hunt you down. Martin Fourcade has long been considered one of if not the fastest skier in World Cup competition history (Johannes Thignes Boe may disagree) and with no misses on the day in the pursuit race, he was undoubtedly yelling "track", the universal signal when overtaking lapped, late starting, or slower skiers, on his way to victory. Germany has proven to be a very successful locale for the French who have won several of the men's and women's pursuit races over the years, a high that Fourcade would feel again at the Ruhpolding pursuit race just one week later.[5]

Antholz-Anterselva, Italy and the Individual Race

Host of biathlon at the 2026 Milano-Cortina XXV Olympic Winter Games and just 175 km south from Ruhpolding near the Austrian border and surrounded by the Reiserferner Massif mountains lies the picturesque valley of Antholz-Anterselva, home to the biathlon stadium situated at the highest altitude (1,634 meters) on the World Cup circuit known as Sudtirol Arena. Sudtirol is a 10 minute walk from the main stadium bus stop which shuttles spectators from a number of local villages in the valley below. As with other venues, ticket holders for the event are provided with a map of the stadium illustrating everything from paths providing access to various locations along skiing loops to where the big screen TV is located near the stadium for watching the action unfold in real time.[11] The Antholz valley has a long history of hosting international competition dating back to 1971 under the management of Paul Zingerle where at the time, the individual race was the only scheduled event. Since then, the stadium has hosted several World Championships and is a regular stop on the World Cup circuit. In preparation for the XXV Olympic Winter Games, major renovations to the tune of $43.9 million are planned and include construction of an underground shooting range.[17]

TWO SKIS AND A RIFLE: AN INTRODUCTION TO BIATHLON

The oldest and most arduous of all competition formats comprising international biathlon, the individual race, is a true test of endurance placing a premium on strong skiing above all else. Biathletes seeking a win assuredly will hope for optimal ski waxing (see Chapter Five) to meet the conditions of the day, for slow skis will unduly fatigue even the strongest of skier. Starting every thirty seconds similar to the sprint event, the individual test begins as each biathlete sets off through the starting gate on a timed run and once out on course they surely will keep an eye on the bib numbers of athletes immediately in sight.[4] They'll know that if a fellow biathlete with a lower starting bib number is passed at any point on the course, the start time difference will be made up by as many places; one place for 30 seconds, two for one minute and so on. But watch out, if passed by an athlete with one higher bib number, they'll just as well know the dejection of now being thirty seconds down on their most recent race rival.

Since there are multiple biathlon events at each venue, skiing loops are color coded for distances and athletes will understand for the individual race to follow the men's brown 4 km and women's yellow 3 km tracks. If the skiing wasn't hard enough and in an ode to the history of the individual race, unlike most other events which have biathletes ski a penalty loop(s) after missing a shot(s), the individual race imposes an even more penal one minute time penalty for each missed shot which is instantly applied and ultimately inflates the athletes overall finishing time.[4] On the morning of February 18th, 2020, Italy's Dorothea Wierer began her individual World Championship quest on home snow, which offers clear advantages in the case of Antholz-Anterselva for Italian national waxing technicians, taking slightly extra time at the range as most athletes do in the individual race to try and shoot clean. Skiing well, Wierer missed a shot each at her initial prone and standing visits to the range incurring 2 minutes of penalty time, yet cleaned her ensuing prone and standing targets. She wasn't alone in missing a shot as only one biathlete out of 98 finishers cleaned all twenty targets on the day. Skiing faster and faster as the race progressed moving from 24th position early to first at the conclusion of the penultimate lap, Wierer, who would rise to the occasion and hold on to win gold in front of a frenzied stadium crowd, undoubtedly and finally cast aside personal struggles in finding success at home.[5]

Image 3.3. A joyous occasion on the 2020 women's 15 km individual race World Championship podium from Antholz-Anterselva. At center is Dorothea Wierer (IT) the newly crowned world champion. To her left is runner-up Vanessa Hinz (GER) and bronze medalist Marte Olsbu Roeiseland (NOR). (Photo by LiveMediaSrl/Shutterstock.com)

Hochfilzen, Austria and the World Championships

No other venue in a non-Olympic year draws as much attention on the World Cup calendar as the World Championships which in 2017 was held at the recently remodeled Hochfilzen biathlon stadium in the Phillerseetal valley of Austria. Hochfilzen, after paying the required 45,000 Euro (≈50,000 USD) application fee and being awarded as host venue, is a routine stop on the World Cup circuit allowing the world's best of the best biathletes plenty of time to prepare for competition. Each nation registers and enters athletes according to a quota determined by their Nations Cup rank from the previous season which is determined by awarding points for individual and relay race placings (e.g., 1st place in an individual competition = 160 pts, 2nd place = 154 pts, and so on) accumulated by all biathletes from a nation over the course of the World Cup season.[4] Top nations, those with great depth of talent, clubs, grass-roots organizations and established training venues, such as Norway, Germany, France (perhaps the big 3), Sweden, Italy, and Russia (as of this writing all athletes and representatives currently banned from participation by the IBU in opposition to the Russia-Ukraine War) annually rank highest in the Nations Cup and send the most biathletes to the World Championships.

Image 3.4. Fans overlooking Hochfilzen biathlon stadium and course at the 2017 IBU World Championships. (Photo by Anrephoto/Shutterstock.com)

After a few days of training to become acquainted with the notoriously tricky shooting conditions that often suddenly arise at Hochfilzen, team Germany struck first by taking the mixed relay gold by only 2.2 seconds over fast closing France and Russia. While the results from the relay and sprint races certainly were front page news in the biathlon world, it would be one family and two seasoned biathletes from the United States who would become the stories of the 2017 World Championships. Having recently been married, 45 year old Ole Einar Bjoerndalen from Norway and multiple Sochi Olympic gold medalist Darya Domracheva from Belarus, less than five months after the birth of their daughter Xenia, would headline the results of the pursuit race. The oldest active at the time and most accomplished international level biathlete ever, Bjoerndalen in defiance of his age would incredibly

TWO SKIS AND A RIFLE: AN INTRODUCTION TO BIATHLON

win his 45th medal at the World Championships taking bronze in the pursuit behind competitors nearly twenty years younger. Not to be outdone and making this a family matter, Domracheva, in her return to the World Cup season and World Championship competition following a year off due to a bout of mononucleosis, would become the surprise of the day by moving up twenty-five places to grab silver in the pursuit race after finishing 27th in the qualifying sprint race held just two days before.[12]

The U.S. men's biathlon team (Lowell Bailey, Leif Nordgren, Tim Burke, and Sean Doherty in this case) awoke on February 16th to bright sunny skies at Hochfilzen and readied themselves for the individual 20 km race as they normally do. The race though, would be anything but ordinary for the United States. Starting with bib #100 and very late in the field of competitors, a risky strategy on a warm and sunny day as the track begins to melt and deteriorate into a slushy snow, Lowell Bailey began skiing his way to an unexpected destiny. The anticipation was palpable as left-handed Bailey started well cleaning his first, second and then third shootings pacing himself as he skied over the undulating course to enter the final shoot just a handful of seconds in front of the best biathletes in the world. Shooting quickly and with a perfect rhythm between shots, the first went down, then two, three...could it be, four, yes five! Slinging the rifle to his back before leaving the range, Bailey would trip the intermediate timing clock six seconds ahead of his closest competitor and needed the ski of his life to maintain that gap to the finish.[13]

The late start strategy seemed to be paying off during Bailey's final lap on the course as the afternoon sun dipped behind the trees casting shadows over the tracks which increases a skier's speed as snow refreezes. Staying within himself despite the crippling fatigue and mental strain of leading a World Championship race, Bailey maintained a natural fluidity in his skiing and the poise of a well-seasoned World Cup competitor. Yet he was slowly losing time out on the course and would be only 2.8 seconds ahead at the 17.2 km time check with less than 3 km to go. The fans knew the spectacle before them and if not rooting their home countryman to a win are surely savvy enough to realize the deep passion these biathletes carry for their sport and will cheer by name any improbable underdog all the way to the finish line. In first place after starting earlier, Ondrej Moravec (CZE) who was watching Bailey on the stadium big screen would shake his head in disbelief as the time gap would shrink to an incredible 0.1 seconds at the 18.9 km time check with just over one kilometer remaining. With adrenaline pumping through his veins Bailey in the final kilometer would, in a perfectly legal and often fortuitous tactic, catch the draft of an earlier Russian starter and moments before the finish line would slingshot around his Russian pacer stretching his left leg forward over the finish line to stop the clock 3.3 seconds ahead of Moravec...victory! Decades in the making and in front of his family, the first ever gold medal at a World Championships for an American would go to an elated yet emotionally and physically exhausted 36 year old Lowell Bailey.[13]

Two days later in the women's mass start event another milestone would be reached by a former All-American cross-country skier turned world-class biathlete. Exuding confidence going into the race, Vermont's Susan Dunklee reflected on how Bailey's strings of success had carried over to the U.S. team.

> I think back to a few years ago when he got his first podium in Kontiolahti [Finland], and I watched him do that. I thought, he has been doing this for a long time and that's possible. Then a week later I got my first podium in Oslo. So that thought crossed my head the other day when he won. I was like, huh, maybe I can feed off of this. You just need to

get some positive momentum going and it makes it easier for the whole team to do well.[14]

Always regarded as one of the fastest skiers on the World Cup circuit, Dunklee left the first shooting with over a five second lead on her closest competitor. In a pattern that would repeat itself seemingly each lap, the pack would catch Dunklee on a large rise out on course, would come together into the shooting range, and be outshot by Dunklee who would once again gap the field to start the next ski loop. She would not be alone though in shooting a perfect 20 for 20 and after leaving the range for the fourth and final time, Dunklee saw on the big stadium screen that she was five seconds in front of then world #1 biathlete, Laura Dahlmeier (GER). Dunklee in her post race interview had a feeling that she might be caught and sure enough, on the highest point out on course, Dahlmeier surged pass in a move that would stick to the finish line. A silver medal in the mass start for journey-woman Dunklee remains the finest accomplishment to date by an American in a sport long dominated by European countries.

Beijing, China: Olympic Trial Run

Thoughts of a state-of-the-art biathlon arena situated amongst a forested and mountainous landscape typically do not gravitate towards the Yin Mountains near Zhangjiakou, a city in the northwestern Hebei province in China. But they certainly did for a trial run World Cup competition in 2021 and again in February 2022 as the Koyangshu Nordic Center and Biathlon Center played host to the XXIV Olympic Winter Games. While smaller in size compared to long standing European venues, Koyangshu's spectator capacity created an intimate experience for those watching any one of the eleven biathlon events including, for only the third time in Olympic history, the mixed relay (the single mixed relay event is part of the World Championships but not on the Olympic program yet). The Norwegian contingency would go on to dominate the Olympic competition results winning more than double the medal count of any other nation overcoming difficult conditions of howling cross winds and bitter cold.

Typically there is a break for athletes following the World Championships which also gives organizers on both ends extra time to prepare for competition and adjust to a six hour time difference at a venue as distant in this case as Asia. Lowell Bailey comments on how his time was spent after the World Championships and leading up to the PyeongChang World Cup trial run; a prelude to the XXIII Winter Olympic Games in South Korea.

> Over the past ten or so days since World Champs I took a few days off to kind of rest, recover and just sort of try to step away from that high-intensity environment. Most of the team members went just outside of Ruhpolding [Germany] and we had a pretty relaxing training camp there. I didn't shoot for the first couple days, and then just tried to get back into my normal routine...we had pretty good travel from Ruhpolding [to PyeongChang], and we came here on the early side compared to a lot of other teams and I think that was an advantage.[15]

To compete and potentially medal in the Olympic Games represents the pinnacle of athletic achievement for many an athlete and for an elite biathlete, it is no different. So when it comes time to showcase the nature of their sport, organizing bodies will work diligently to ensure that an Olympic venue has undertaken all necessary preparations well in advance. The IBU thus in a move traditionally made the year prior to the Olympics decided to trial run a World Cup event in late February 2021 at Koyangshu, which had seen some delays in construction due to its remote location, in anticipation of the Olympics to come.

The pressure shouldered by athletes leading up to and after the World Championships leaves some reluctant to travel to venues scheduled some distance away. On occasion, the World Cup will work its way to other continents, and as recently as the 2023/2024 season two events were held on North American snow at Canmore, Alberta, Canada and Soldier Hollow, Utah. Some years ago during the 2015/2016 season, several top Norwegian biathletes, even before the World Championships had occurred in Oslo, Norway, decided against crossing the pond for the North American World Cup competitions and the 2017 PyeongChang World Cup (a trial run for the XXIII Olympics in 2018) would be no different. Yet despite the more demanding travel logistics and difficult conditions of traveling to North America, South Korea, or even Beijing, more and more athletes are reluctant to give up potential World Cup points and tough out the journey to gain experience on a newly constructed biathlon course, particularly in the build-up to an Olympic year.

Image 3.5. The Alpensia Biathlon Center played host to eleven individual and team events at the XXIII Winter Olympic Games in PyeongChang, South Korea. (Photo by KoreaKHW/Shutterstock.com)

Kontiolahti, Finland and Oslo Holmenkollen, Norway: Scandinavian Regulars

Mid- to late-March brings warmer spring-like temperatures to the lower latitude venues on the World Cup circuit, yet the relatively shorter days in Finland and Norway mean consistently cooler evenings and less snow melt. An annual World Cup stop, Kontiolahti is located within the easternmost region of North Karelia near the capital city of Joensuu 438 km northeast of Helsinki and would play an unlikely World Cup host in 2017. It's not as if Kontiolahti hasn't hosted large scale international biathlon in the past, in fact the event park has been a regular stop for the World Cup over the past twenty years. However, Kontiolahti became a last minute host after an IBU emergency Executive Committee's decision to relocate the originally scheduled venue of Tyumen, Russia. This came after implications that the Russian Biathlon Union knew of state-sponsored Russian doping outlined in the World Anti-Doping Association (WADA) commissioned and jaw dropping McLaren Report (see Chapter Seven). The International Olympic Committee (IOC) has further recommended that winter sporting bodies, such as IBU, refuse to award major events to countries out of compliance with WADA regulations. Nevertheless and despite these serious allegations of systematic doping in Russia, Tyumen was the last venue on the World Cup schedule as recently as the 2018.[16]

As the season draws to a close on the World Cup schedule, the competition proves fierce as individual athletes strive to win a race or one of the season-long competitions and teams push for national recognition and Nations Cup points. Every world class biathlete dreams of hoisting the crystal globe overhead as recognition for being the most consistently high placed finisher in the individual biathlon disciplines including the mass start, individual, sprint, and pursuit. The most prized trophy is for the overall World Cup total points which recognizes the biathlete who performs best in all individual disciplines combined. Whoever wins the crystal globe for total points has every right to call her or himself the best biathlete in the world. Similarly, the relay events, including the mixed described earlier, and team relay which incorporates a shooting format that is no different than the mixed relay events pitting four female or male biathletes from each country against one another over individual distances of 6 km and 7.5 km (e.g., 4 x 6 km and 4 x 7.5 km), respectively, also award season ending trophies to the most consistent nations.[4] A highlight at the 2017 Kontiolahti World Cup would be the combined efforts of Dunklee and Bailey who teamed up for the single mixed relay event to best such powerhouses as Germany and France for a silver winning performance; which remains the best ever U.S. finish in the event to date.[5]

Image 3.6. Gabriela Koukalova (née Soukalova) holding the crystal globe for winning the total points World Cup competition in 2016. (Photo by VOJTa Herout/Shutterstock.com)

Oslofjord provides a most captivating view as it stretches 120 km from north to south and marks the entrance to the capital city of Oslo and the Holmenkollen biathlon arena, frequently the final World Cup stop. A sense of renewed energy permeates the atmosphere as biathletes feel that despite a season-long accumulation of fatigue from travel and competition there is one more chance at glory. No one would take this to heart more in 2017 than Finland's Mari Laukkanen a journey-women biathlete who in her lengthy career had so far been on the World Cup podium just once before. Opening the competition at Holmenkollen would be the women's 7.5 km sprint where Laukkanen, who started early wearing bib #7, set off to an astounding tempo. In many a case, an athlete can start too fast and enter the range with a less than desirable heart rate and breathing tempo only to find themselves struggling with a wandering shooting focus. Perhaps though in this case the world had forgotten that Laukkanen, like several others on the biathlon World Cup circuit, had often been invited to represent her nation in cross-country skiing events giving credit to her world class speed. She would go on to clean both shooting stops to far surpass her 70% hit rate on the season commenting after the race that "Today I feel fantastic. Two clean bouts, I should do that more often. It's a great feeling!"[12] No one would catch her on the day.

...

Every World Cup season starts off with media listing several contenders for an individual crystal globe, yet in the end, only a select few can realistically expect to be holding the trophy. The 2019/2020 season would see 93 and 95 different women and men, respectively, earn World Cup points in the 21 total scored competitions; a shortened season due to the COVID-19 pandemic and subsequent cancellation of World Cup stop #10 in Oslo, Holmenkollen. In the end, there are only a few individuals who are handed crystal globes for their consistent performances in each discipline and no one would find more success than Italian Dorothea Wierer and Norwegian Johannes Thignes Boe, who has gone on to win every World Cup total score bar one since the 2018/2019 season. From 2016-2018 in what could be described as one of the finest run of performances in World Cup history, Fourcade would win the crystal globe for all five individual competitions; individual, mass start, sprint, pursuit, and the biggest of them all, total points. On reflection, he would comment "I never imagined a [2016/2017] season like it. It's the best season in biathlon ever and honestly I didn't think it was possible!" Finding her own success over the same season would be Germany's Laura Dahlmeier and after clinching the total points in Kontiolahti would remark "It is amazing, I have no words. It is such a dream come true at this moment; just amazing!" Dahlmeier would go on to split the remaining crystal globes with Gabriela Koukalova, the previous year's total points winner, securing the individual and pursuit titles to Koukalova's mass start and sprint titles.[12]

If before reading this book you would have thought Norway or another Scandinavian country would dominate team biathlon competitions and be considered the best country in the world, you'd partially be right. With five team crystal globes on offer, Germany has long dominated the men's and women's Nations Cup points and relay events until Norway as recently as 2017/2018 has assumed the right to claim themselves as the premier biathlon nation in the world. France should never be discounted and is always in the Nations Cup and relay races mix as the 'big three' countries, with Sweden knocking on the door, continue to set the standard for elite world-class biathlon performance. With the XXV Winter Olympic Games on the horizon, the sport of biathlon remains as popular as ever and the upcoming World Cup season and beyond should be very exciting indeed.

Chapter Four
On Being a World Class Biathlete

Years of hard work, a strong support structure, a modicum of talent, and perhaps a dash of luck along the way provide the ingredients to make a successful biathlete. Virtually all athletes competing at the World Cup level have this recipe down; this is not a family secret held closely from one generation to the next. The top 1% of international-level biathletes, the elite of the elite, further add their own secret sauce to the mix and add their name in a historical context as a legend of the sport. From the early years of limited competition (e.g., only the individual race was competed at the 1960 Winter Olympics) to the current and expansive World Cup, few enter the conversation of being considered the best biathlete of all time. But if not for the parity of today's World Cup competition, there would not be opportunity for a Justin Braisaz-Bouchet (FRA), Johannes Thignes Boe (NOR), Elvira Oeberg (SWE), or Benedikt Doll (GER) to shine.

For most, the journey to reach the World Cup begins at the minor leagues equivalent IBU Cup. Held at venues apart from the World Cup, IBU Cup biathletes from many a nation seek to earn qualifying points during the season to gain the right to be 'called up' to the big leagues. Additional points are on offer during the annual biathlon Open European Championships, the IBU Cup equivalent of the top tier World Championships. A complicated system of points earned from sprint and individual IBU Cup competitions plugged into a regression-like equation, determines eligibility to compete at the World Cup level.

IBU Qualifying Points = ((athlete's time/winners time)-1) x Race Factor + Race Penalty

The race factor is a fixed number set by the IBU at 800 and the race penalty, essentially a handicap for lower placings, is determined by summing the points of the top three ranked athletes in the IBU Cup up to the most recent competition, divided by 3.75. Points for individual placings in an IBU Cup or equivalent level sprint or individual race are determined on a sliding scale where first place awards 90 points, second place is worth 75 points, while third is good for 60 points, and so on down to 40th place.[1] In what may seem paradoxical, the lower the actual calculated IBU qualifying points, the better.

Let's take an example of two athletes having competed in an IBU Cup sprint race from a recent season. The top 3 finishers, all of whom were in the top ten points at the time, at a developmental IBU Cup race in Beitostolen, Norway were Vetle Sjaastad Christiansen (NOR; now an Olympian; 26:56.6), Roman Rees (GER; a fixture on the World Cup circuit; 27:13.1) and Vegard Gjermundshaug (NOR; 27:43.1) and let's compare the IBU qualifying points earned by Rees and Gjermundshaug for this race.[2] Plugging Rees' time into the IBU qualifying points equation gives us:

((27:13.1 or 27.22/26:56.6 or 26.94) -1) x Race Factor (800) + Race Penalty (90+75+60/3.75) = <u>68.32 pts</u>

Doing the same for Gjermundshaug:

((27:43.1 or 27.72/26.94) – 1) x (RF) 800 + (RP) = <u>83.16 pts</u>

Both Rees' and Gjermundshaug's placings and times relative to the winner are excellent results and to be eligible to compete on the World Cup, athletes must undertake at least one race at the level of an IBU Cup, World Championships, Open European Championships, or Olympic Winter Games and earn 125 IBU qualifying points or less. In the case of Rees and Gjermundshaug, both would qualify for the top tier IBU World Cup on this IBU Cup race alone. Simply qualifying does not guarantee that a national federation will call up an IBU Cup biathlete; that is far from the case in nations with deep talent pools like Norway, Russia, and Germany and remaining on the World Cup circuit is a different and more daunting story altogether. In fact, such is the depth of the Norwegian squad that multiple World Cup winner and Olympic gold medalist Vetle Sjaastad Christiansen (NOR), easily capable of being a top biathlete on most any other national team, was relegated to the IBU Cup at the conclusion of the first trimester during the 2023/2024 season.[35]

Apart from the single competition World Cup qualifying criteria, athletes must have 150 qualifying points or less, using both the same sliding points scale for placing in a sprint or individual race as well as the IBU qualifying points formula, at the end of the last trimester in order to remain on the World Cup circuit the following year. The World Cup consists of three trimesters with three events per trimester, usually World Cups 1-3, 4-6, and 7-9. Averaging a biathletes top three best results in the sprint and individual competitions at the end of the last trimester of competition, normally World Cup events 7-9 on the schedule, and plugging those results into yet another formula determines if qualifying points are sufficiently *low* enough to maintain good standing on the World Cup circuit. After five trimesters with no points scored, a biathlete is removed from a nation's World Cup eligibility list and may be sent down to the IBU Cup. Convoluted yes, but basically the more consistently high placed a biathlete finishes in World Cup sprint and other individual competitions throughout each trimester, the more likely they will continue to race on the premier circuit.

Earning the necessary 180 qualifying points for the World Championships and Olympics is seemingly on paper less stringent than the World Cup; however, the number of competitors invited to these premier events is limited by nation based on current Nations Cup points. For example, the top five countries in the season ending Nations Cup competition, teams such as Norway, Russia, Germany and France who consistently have biathletes placing in the top 10% of World Cup races, may in the following season register eight and start six biathletes in any number of races at a single World Cup venue. That starting number drops to four biathletes at the World Championships and perhaps even fewer at the Olympic Winter Games, where the final quota is arranged between the IOC and IBU, bestowing on these events a premier and elite 'member-only' status on the competition calendar.[1]

...

Any top biathlete will be the first to acknowledge that individual success would be impossible without the support of teammates and staff and after her success at the World Championships in 2017, Susan Dunklee reflected, "We have staff who have worked for decades believing this level is possible. Now the door has been opened. I don't think they will have to wait decades for the next relay medals or World Championships podium." The "we" that Dunklee mentions refers to the staff, coaches and leadership of US Biathlon, the IBU internationally recognized biathlon federation of the United States.[3] Founded in 1980, the U.S. Biathlon Association's mission is to promote the growth of biathlon in the U.S. and to prepare athletes for international competition, including the World Cup and Olympics.[4]

Well before and in anticipation of the 1960 Winter Olympics in Squaw Valley, the U.S. Army established the first training center in the United States at Fort Richardson near Anchorage, Alaska. However, after budget constraints following the Vietnam War, Fort Richardson would close its doors in the late 70's. With the 1980 Lake Placid, New York Winter Olympics looming on the horizon, attention to organizing the biathlon events would turn to members of the Vermont National

Guard. The sport of biathlon would finally spark the curiosity of the casual observer and would not only lead to the formation of the U.S. Biathlon Association but provide impetus to the Vermont National Guard members to establish a biathlon facility at the Ethan Allen Firing Range in Jericho, Vermont. As John Morton, former American Olympian and 2008 U.S. Biathlon Hall of Fame inductee relives:

> Over the past three decades, that facility, and the support of the Vermont National Guard have, to a significant degree, filled the void left by the closing of the Fort Richardson training center. The Ethan Allen Biathlon Center boasts one of the finest biathlon competition venues in the country, and has hosted several major events, including international military competitions and Junior Biathlon World Championships. Perhaps equally as noteworthy, the Vermont National Guard facility has inspired dozens of young athletes to try the sport, several of whom have earned national attention.[5]

Several of America's strongest ever biathletes, including Lowell Bailey (now Director of High Performance for U.S. Biathlon) and Susan Dunklee, have ties to Vermont, as did former president and CEO of U.S. Biathlon Max Cobb (currently Jack Giehart), and Algis Shalna, recently (2023) retired Eastern Regional Coach and former Soviet Olympic gold medalist in the biathlon relay.[4,5,36]

Once in Europe, coaches, staff, and athletes generally stay put, or perhaps in the case of the Americans or Canadians, occasionally returning home to North America for a short break following the World Championships. Most will remain in Europe for training camps (see Chapter Seven) between World Cups to fine tune fitness and shooting technique. A strong support staff for the biathletes keeps the gears turning smoothly in a sport with several moving parts; travel, ski and rifle maintenance, lodging, meals, and physical and psychological training. For the Olympics such as Sochi, Russia in 2014, Norway sent a full contingent of coaches and staff to support their Olympians including a sports director, six coaches and six wax technicians.[6] The United States national team, which registered one fewer male and female biathlete each than Norway due to Nations Cup points standings, sent then German transplant and team leader Bernd Eisenbichler, head men's coach Per Nilsson (Sweden), women's head coach Jonne Kahkonnen, Italian coach Armin Auchentaller (now the national team head coach), and four ski/wax technicians including a designated grinder (see Chapter Five). A medical doctor, physiotherapist (Physical Therapist equivalent in the U.S.), sport psychologist and press officer completed the team cohort, many of whom were in Sochi because of funding by the United States Olympic Committee (USOC) in an effort to hire world-class and high performance coaching and staff to win a first biathlon Olympic medal.[4,7] Under the direction of Per Nilsson, the United States took major steps forward in developing Team USA on the international level and saw athletes like Tim Burke, Susan Dunklee and Lowell Bailey consistently performing at the highest level of international competition. Since then, U.S. Biathlon has undergone structural reorganization to its athlete/sport performance and development programs and a refinement of coaching responsibilities to continue this promising trajectory in the sport.

Operating on a comparatively slim 2.9 million dollar annual budget[8], the Americans' performances of recent are all the more impressive and reveal the dedication that athletes and staff have for their craft. Team Russia on the other hand, a program of similar magnitude to Germany, France, and Norway, are said to operate on budgets approaching ten times what the United States realizes from the USOC, IBU, television broadcasting, prize money, ski, clothing and ammunition sponsors, and corporate and individual donations. From the perspective of an athlete, Lowell Bailey explains just why the United States has yet to find Olympic glory.

> If you're a corporation in Europe, it's a better choice to sponsor a biathlete than say a basketball player or baseball player, because you're going to get more TV time. So I think that's why it's so tough for us to break onto the medals stand because we're fighting a little bit of an uphill battle.[9]

Max Cobb explains that a biathlete like Unites States' Tim Burke, a perennial top twenty finisher in individual events and one-time winner of a silver medal at the 2013 World Championships, can earn a less then princely $50,000-$60,000 annually[10] whereas top athletes, like now retired Laura Dahlmeier or Martin Fourcade, live quite well and bank several times that on national federation salaries and sponsorship money, not to mention prize money for top finishes on the World Cup or bonuses for Olympic gold which can exceed $150,000. Yet there are considerable demands from sponsors, who reap the rewards of increased sales by instilling a win on Sunday sell on Monday mentality, as Dahlmeier explains.

> Naturally, they want to fit in as many meetings with me as they possibly can. My main sponsor Viessman – along with my other partners, including DKB, Kornspitz, Joka (Waffe), and Adidas – is always inviting me to discussions and events, especially during world cups. Of course, they also like it when I share things on social media. I try to satisfy them as much as I can. A post on Instagram here, a post on Facebook there – I always have to take care that my athletic achievements don't suffer.[11]

But like Dahlmeier, many work in the offseason to supplement their income when sponsorship money, national federation stipends, and prize money run dry. Dahlmeier for one has worked as a customs staff sergeant in the Austrian Federal Armed Forces, while Tim Burke took on the task of personally reaching out to patrons "through a cold call or cold email, I've probably been turned down 100 times."[10] IBU prize money for placings in individual races (sprint, mass start, pursuit, etc.) falls away quickly from the top, where the gap between 1st place at €15,000 ($16,400) and 10th place at €3,250 ($3,500) is considerable. Further prize money after each race for the yellow race bib wearing overall world cup leader (€1,000 per bib awarded) and to those wearing a red individual competition leader bib (e.g., €750 per mass start, pursuit, sprint and individual competition leaders) can't be relied upon either to entirely supplement income since two or three biathletes tend to dominate these internal competitions.[1] Fortunately, in a move by the executive board of IBU and beginning with the 2022/2023 season, prize money for placing in individual competitions increased from the top 20 to now 30 athletes and is set to undergo another revision for 2024-2026.[31] Even so, the driving force for these athletes is not money but rather a love and passion for the sport in the ultimate quest for personal and national glory.

...

At the final 2017 World Cup in Oslo, Norway, Martin Fourcade undertook preparations for the 15 km mass start race as usual with one small oversight; he forgot to load his ammunition clips with bullets, which are subsequently carried on the rifle. Skiing into the range for the first time as if everything was normal, Fourcade would drop into the prone position and in horror only then realize the error. With no bullets, he would raise his hand for help and reacting fastest to the situation would be his coach who would toss him a clip from behind the barriers. This fiasco would cost Fourcade only a few seconds after he regrouped and hit all the targets but the real drama to follow would be that what his coach had done was strictly forbidden because by rule the shooting range is considered a no coaching zone. Fourcade (or the coach really) should have waited for the range official to hand him spare clips as needed. Instead Fourcade would have to continue racing with an asterisk next to his name, a sign that the race jury and technical delegate would deliberate on whether or not a disqualification or time penalty would be in order.[3]

The competition jury has a presence at all major international biathlon competitions and are appointed to act as an authority on all matters related to the event. The scope of the competition jury's purview ranges from checking the eligibility of all competitors entered in a race to stopping a race if, for example, severe weather conditions endanger the correct conduct of competition. With a charge of ensuring fairness and correct procedures, the jury may often not witness a rules violation and will only learn of potential wrongdoing after a national federation has filed a formal protest. Fortunately for spectators who desire real-time race results, protests from a national federation must be filed within fifteen minutes after the conclusion of the race to be considered by the competition jury.[1] Fourcade knew he was under investigation but decided to keep racing as usual realizing he would learn of his fate after the race had been completed.[3] He would go on to clean all four shooting stages and win the race by a comfortable seventeen second margin yet was unsure if the results would stand.[2]

After breaking the timing light at the finish line, Fourcade, just as with all other competitors, would remove his skis and immediately pass through a finish equipment/materials inspection area where an IBU official as a safety precaution slides the rifle bolt to open the firing chamber making sure no bullets remain chambered. After clearing the inspection, athletes enter a fenced off 'mixed zone' where TV broadcasting and other media are stationed to interview athletes who still have the race fresh in their minds, undoubtedly asking Fourcade about 'ammunitiongate'. Continuing through the finish line maze, athletes pass a refreshment area that is "protected against the introduction of any prohibited substances" and finally are greeted by coaches and staff and retrieve dry/warm clothing for a change under the privacy of a "change shelter."[1]

The competition jury would be seen on TV deliberating for several minutes while fans anxiously awaited a decision, any decision. In the end, the jury adjudicated to not take action against Fourcade or his team as Lowell Bailey rationalized, "I think the jury was right. I've been there. I know what it's like to make a simple, costly mistake, and I think he definitely didn't gain any advantage by NOT loading his clips."[3] And in a true gesture of the spirit of competition and sport, Germany's Simon Schempp who was leading the World Cup mass start points competition and wearing the red bib at the start of the race in Oslo, did not instruct the German National Federation to file a protest, which if upheld, would have awarded him the crystal globe! By placing first in the race to Shempp's 20th position, Fourcade would overtake the German in the points for the mass start and win his fifth and final crystal globe in a remarkable season.[3]

With the outcome of the race deemed official, the top athletes on the day are invited to a flower ceremony held in front of the Holmenkollen stadium where each athlete lines up adjacent to the podium while the official hymn of the IBU plays in the background. As the crowd cheers exuberantly, the first placed biathlete is called in the native tongue of the host venue and then in English, followed by second and so on until up to six positions in a World Cup event are announced over the loud speaker. Carrying their skis, poles and rifle to the podium, undoubtedly appeasing sponsors, the athletes exchange high fives and are bestowed with flowers, a medal, and even local presents, such as a blanket or gift basket filled with local fare. Often, athletes will throw their flowers into the crowd and sign autographs as a thank you to fans for their always boisterous and never derogatory support. The top three podium placers are quickly whisked away after the flower ceremony to an IBU required media interview where Fourcade would remark, "I wanted to thank and to give all my respect to the team of Germany and to Simon Schempp, who decided to not ask for a protest. That's a big gesture. I really take my hat off to Simon Schempp. I must say how impressed I am by their class, they deserve much more than a crystal globe today."[3]

...

The rare few who can expect to win on any given day, or even those that do, seem to possess a combination of traits; a perseverance in spirit despite extreme bodily fatigue that threatens to overwhelm the mind, a characteristic and flawless grace when skiing, an air of calmness and familiarity during shooting, never seemingly being hurried or panicked on the race course, an unwavering poise in the heat of competition, and an ability to narrow focus away from surrounding distractions. The peerless few who have consistently race after race and year after year emanated these attributes will go down in history as the best the sport has ever seen.

Magdalena Neuner (Germany)

Born on February 9th, 1987 in the German alpine resort town of Garmisch-Partenkirchen, Magdalena "Lena" Neuner would take to skiing not long after she could walk at four years of age and would start competing as a biathlete at her local ski club SC Wallgau at age nine. Between the ages of 12-15, Neuner would win 29 races at the biathlon Students Cup of the German Ski Association and claim the overall title four times. The following year, she would win the German Cup at 16 years old which paved the way for her inclusion on the European Cup competitions where she would win on four occasions.[12] With such early success in Europe, she would be invited as an official representative of Germany for the 2004 Junior/Youth World Championships in Haute Maurienne, France where she would take home one silver and two gold medals. Her rise to stardom would continue one year later at the 2005 Junior/Youth World Championships in Kontiolahti, Finland with two silvers and a gold in the sprint race begging the question when she would make her debut on the World Cup circuit.[2]

Only months later on January 13th, 2006 at the Ruhpolding, Germany World Cup, Neuner would debut to a respectable 41st place in the sprint race and afterwards would go on to compete at nine more World Cup venues that season. Still considered a junior, Magdalena would participate once more at the 2006 Junior World Championships held in Presque Isle, Maine, where she would rather dominate the competition by winning two golds and a silver medal. After just one season on the World Cup circuit, Neuner would return for the 2006/2007 season and win her first race in Oberhof, Germany receiving noteworthy media attention in front of a partisan home crowd. That first win would be the catalyst for one relay and two individual gold medals at the 2007 World Championships in Antholz, Italy, and a full four more victories on the World Cup in a season never anticipated nor equaled by a 20 year old merely one season after her rookie year.[2,12]

In a career nothing short of phenomenal that would run through the 2011/2012 season, Magdalena would rack up 34 World Cup victories, three overall World Cup titles, and twelve World Championship and two Olympic gold medals. She will be remembered as one of the fastest skiers setting best course times in 66 World Cup races and placing in the top three fastest skiers in no fewer than 77% of all races started. Her career shooting statistics are nearly as impressive at 78% career accuracy, which from the beginning steadily improved in subsequent World Cup seasons.[2] Neuner, wishing for a normal life and despite a relatively short career, retired from competition after the 2012 Khanty-Mansiysk mass start race. She currently resides with her husband and daughter in Wallgau, Bavaria.

Ole Einar Bjoerndalen (Norway)

Often referred to as "The King of Biathlon", Ole Einar Bjoerndalen was born on January 27th, 1974 and even at 43 years old was still incredulously competing at the highest level on the World Cup circuit. Bjoerndalen was born the fourth of five children to a farmer and housewife near the industrial city of Drammen, Norway. He would first become interested in biathlon at ten years of age competing alongside his older brother Dag. Spending his athletic time between cross-country skiing and biathlon, Ole at 17 years would finally settle on the latter mentioning his existence during those times helped focus his efforts "coming from a simple family with a lot of training when I was young" created "the right atmosphere around you growing up."[13]

At 18 years of age, Bjoerndalen would make his international debut at the Junior World Championships and while placing well outside the medals would in the eyes of many exhibit great promise. The following year that promise would bear fruit with Ole winning three out of four possible gold medals at the 1993 Junior World Championships and gaining selection by Norway to compete in the 1994 Winter Olympic Games in Lillehammer, Norway. Following the '93 Junior World Championships, Bjoerndalen would make his World Cup debut in March 1993 hence beginning an ironman-like career that would extend for 25 years.[13] While competing, Ole and his wife Darya Domracheva, a multiple World Cup and Olympic gold medal winning biathlete in her own right, travelled together with their daughter Xenia on the World Cup circuit in a large RV, equipped with an indoor skate skiing treadmill.

As prolific a career the sport has ever seen, it is prudent to describe Bjoerndalen's World Cup and Olympic accomplishments separately for the simple reason that each remains unrivaled to this day. When reviewing all of the individual races that he has competed in, his rivals would be disheartened to learn that if Ole lined up to start, he would win every fourth race. In the years between 1998-2016, he would taste victory twenty times in an individual or team event race at the World Championships and in combination with his World Cup performances, Ole would amass a total of 95 individual wins; the pursuit race being his strongest discipline. Add to these results a crystal globe for each of his six overall and twenty individual event World Cup competition titles and you are left with the single most impressive CV in the history of the sport.[2]

Considered the greatest Winter Olympian regardless of the sport, Bjoerndalen had plans to line up for his seventh Winter Olympics in PyeongChang in 2018 but was not selected by Norway for lack of recent race success. His tally of thirteen Olympic medals, eight being gold, remains unrivaled in an Olympic career dating back to the 1994 Lillehammer Games. Since winning gold in the sprint race at Nagano, Japan in 1998, Bjoerndalen has only once missed out on the top podium step once at the 2006 Turin Games. It has been written that "his remarkable success, consistency and longevity are, in large measure, due to a peerless level of professionalism. He has pushed his sport to physical limits never seen before, with meticulous preparation and a punishing regime that has seen him clock up 900-1,000 training hours every year from the age of 15."[14] Reporters have even joked that after a win, he celebrates by riding a stationary bike. Such is Bjoerndalen's legendary focus on preparing for competition as Tim Burke points out that others had to adapt or die. "He's single handedly changed the sport. He really turned it into a professional sport, in the late '90s, I would say. He's very innovative, and he became so dominant that everyone else had to react to the way he was training to be competitive."[13]

A 1,000 pound bronze statue has been erected in Bjoerndalen's honor to the delight of King Harald V, but he was not ready to hang up his skis just yet. His first reaction when seeing the statue in his hometown of Simostranda, Norway was "I'm not dead yet! My career isn't over yet!" When he did arrive in PyeongChang, it was in a new role as coach of the Belarusian contingent of biathletes, not least of whom was Domracheva herself. Bjoerndalen has owed his longevity to "the sport has never been a job for me. Always a hobby."[13] And when Ole did finally retire from competition in 2018, the world of biathlon lost one of its greatest competitors ever and gained a most respected and hallowed ambassador. In fact, both he and Darya became the head and women's coaches for the Chinese biathlon team just as the countdown began for the Beijing 2022 Winter Olympic Games compelling Ole to remark that "this is a dream job because I loved my sport as an athlete."[32]

Image 4.1. Bjoerndalen in the pursuit race trailing his Norwegian compatriot Johannes Thignes Boe with Lowell Bailey in 3rd position; IBU World Championships 2017. (Photo by Anrephoto/Shutterstock.com)

Magdalena Forsberg (Sweden)

On paper alone, Magdalena Forsberg's career has been every bit as successful as Neuner's, even surpassing her Norwegian neighbor's World Cup victory total of 34 wins. Forsberg was born on July 25th, 1967 as Magdalena Wallin in Ullanger, Vasternorrland County, Sweden. Coming to the sport as many do, Forsberg initially started her career as a cross-country skier and was a member of the Swedish National Team for several years from 1988 to the early '90s. Finding a modicum of success in cross-country skiing, Magdalena gave up the sport after an achilles tendon injury kept her from competing in the

1994 Olympics and afterwards she would turn her attention to biathlon. As a child her father, Jan, took Magdalena moose hunting teaching her the skills of handling a rifle and would later express that she was only interested in biathlon for fun, and not for the prizes or financial remuneration.[15] Her skiing prowess conveyed well to biathlon and finding encouragement from her future husband Henrik she would make her World Cup debut on December 8th, 1994.

"I had to ask, who is this person? This cannot be me." Forsberg would recall from an interview those unassuming words after winning a 7.5 km sprint race and placing 5th in the overall World Cup points competition in her rookie 1994/1995 season.[15] The 1995/1996 season would find herself with similar albeit modest success after winning the 15 km individual race in Holmenkollen. The world would only have to wait until the following year for what could be considered her truly breakout season. With four individual wins in 1996/1997, Magdalena would begin to accumulate more World Cup victories than any other woman in the history of the sport. Her 2000/2001 season will be remembered as arguably the best in history after an unprecedented 14 victories including two World Championship gold medals in the individual and mass start races. Until her retirement at the conclusion of the 2001/2002 season, all told Magdalena would win 42 times on the World Cup circuit including six golds at the World Championships as well as the overall points competition a record six times.[2] The only blemish on an otherwise consummate resume would be a lack of Olympic gold where she would twice win bronze for her efforts in the individual and sprint events at Salt Lake City. Forsberg has had an active presence in the sport since retirement and featured as a commentator for Eurosport's PyeongChang 2018 Olympic biathlon coverage.[16]

Martin Fourcade (France)

Perhaps the most talented all-around biathlete the world has yet to be acquainted with reached the pinnacle of a superlative career as recently as 2017/2018 and still we witnessed him winning races and/or crystal globes in the seasons to follow. Martin is the middle of three brothers born to Gisele and Marcel Fourcade of Ceret, France on September 14th, 1988. Martin took up biathlon in 2002 following in the ski tracks of his elder brother Simon who as well competed for the French national biathlon team and on the World Cup circuit until his retirement in 2019. After competing for France at the 20 07 and 2008 Junior World Championships, Martin would make the jump to the World Cup debuting at Oslo in March, 2008, in his only appearance that season. In his first full season the following year, Fourcade would be in the points at several races and secure a 4th place highlight in the World Championship relay event. Martin would only have to wait until the next season for his first of many wins to come. Claiming victory in the pursuit race at Kontiolahti, Fourcade would follow that with a pursuit victory in Oslo securing by one point the overall pursuit World Cup title for the 2009/2010 season.[2]

Fourcade's rise to stardom would continue into the 2010/2011 season with mass starts wins at Antholz and Fort Kent (USA) prior to entering the World Championships in Khanty-Mansiysk, Russia. After a bronze in the mixed relay, and silver in the sprint, he would claim his first of many World Championship gold medals in the pursuit race by skiing faster than any of his competitors. He would cement his status as the best in the sport the following season by winning no fewer than eight times on the World Cup circuit, including the overall World Cup title and three individual gold medals at the World Championships, a feat achieved by only two other biathletes, Ole Einar Bjoerndalen (2005 and 2009) and Raphaël Poirée (2004). Demonstrating that the 2011/

2012 season was no fluke, Martin backed that up with a ten win season in 2012/2013 and more impressively, became at the time only the second man in history (Raphaël Poirée before and Johannes Thignes Boe since; Bjoerndalen almost accomplished the feat during the 2004/2005 season) to win the overall World Cup and all discipline titles in the same year.[2] Such was his skiing prowess that Fourcade was selected to represent France at a World Cup ski only race in Sweden. Commenting on the experience, he later reflected "I didn't know what kind of result I could expect, but it was a good goal and a good idea for me to compete in a cross-country race. I'm not satisfied of the result and I think it's not my real level. But sometimes you go down in order to go higher."[17] In fact, Martin has long been the fastest skier on the biathlon World Cup circuit besting his closest rivals at times by more than 0.5% and the field by nearly 4% which translates into several seconds per lap in any given race.[18]

When the 2014 Winter Olympic Games in Sochi were looming, Fourcade started the 2013/2014 season well by winning an individual and sprint race in Ostersund. On the final lead up to the Olympics he would stumble and fail to make a significant impression at the Antholz World Cup after taking the prior week off from competition. All athletes feel an extra sense of pressure at the Olympics, but Fourcade would rise to the occasion in the pursuit race. Leading into the final shooting stage of the race, Martin entered the range fully aware of the importance his accuracy would have. Shot after shot found its target, and after the last hit its mark, he would stretch out his arm fist pumping in the air after realizing that no one would catch him on the final lap.[19] Fourcade would continue his good fortune into the individual race where he would capture his second gold of the Games.

From 2014 to as recently as 2018, Martin would be the dominant figure in men's biathlon winning the World Cup overall title every year and all individual discipline titles three years running. In 2016, he matched and then surpassed his compatriot Raphaël Poirée to move into second place on the all-time World Cup win list with 47 victories. Asked about his accomplishments in a post-race interview, "Today I joined Raphaël Poirée with the number of World Cup wins; that means a lot for me. I grew up watching Raphaël on TV. To join legends you need to [be] inspired, and I know how much he inspired me."[20] After successes over the past few seasons, Fourcade announced his retirement from competition on March 13th, 2020 and will be remembered as one of the most decorated biathletes ever, behind only legend Ole Einar Bjoerndalen in overall individual victories, with 83 World Cup and Olympic wins to his credit.[33]

Highly Honorable Mentions

Spanning a career from 1967-1980, **Alexander Tikhonov** became one of the most successful biathletes of all time, and as William Frank[21] writes, he was "the consummate communist, the very embodiment of the socialist camp's notion of the sport, and arguably one of the most recognizable athletes in the Soviet Union."(231) Tikhonov would win eleven World Championship (five individual) and four Olympic gold medals (all four in team relay events) in those 13 years of international competition placing him 4th all-time on the men's most victories list for these two showcase events.[22] He would become head of the Russian Biathlon Union and Vice President of the IBU in 2002. In 2007 Tikhonov would be accused and convicted of conspiring to poison a regional governor but was granted a parliamentary amnesty in celebration of the 55th anniversary of the Soviet victory in World War II.[23] Tikhonov later would be a part of the management team for the

Russian Biathlon Union, now suspended and under the direction of Victor Maigurov.

Ursula "Uschi" Disl began cross-country skiing at age 10 and soon found that skate skiing was more to her liking. At age 16 she made the switch to biathlon and in 1990 at the age of 20 would join the German national team. Nicknamed "Turbo-Disl" for her swift skiing, no doubt owing to her cross-country skiing background, Uschi would dominate international biathlon for 16 years winning eight World Championships and nine Olympic medals.[24] She remains 4th on the all-time World Cup victories list and while many of her preeminent wins were the result of a team effort, Disl won 30 individual events from 1990-2006.[2] In 2005, Disl became the first biathlete to ever be awarded German Sportswoman of the Year.

Emil Hegle Svendsen would be recognized as Norway's greatest male biathlete if not for the existence of Ole Einar Bjoerndalen and recent ascendancy of Johannes Thignes Boe. Active on the World Cup circuit until 2018, Emil first made an impression on the biathlon world at 19 years of age at the Haute Maurienne Junior World Championships where he won gold in the pursuit race. Following one more year at the Junior World's, Svendsen would make his World Cup debut for the 2005/2006 season. Two years would pass before Emil would win an individual race, not once, but on six occasions over the 2007/2008 season. He won two individual and team gold medals at the Olympics, 12 World Championship wins (five individual), 38 World Cup individual races, four individual discipline World Cup titles, and the overall World Cup points title on one occasion.[2] Emil is based in Trondheim, Norway, and skis for the Trondheim Skiskyterre ski club.[25]

After striking gold in the 15 km individual race at the 2010 Vancouver Winter Games, a first in women's biathlon and the 100th all-time for

Norway, **Tora Berger** will be remembered as Norway's finest female biathlete. Tora was born in Ringerike and grew up in the mountainous terrain of Lesjla, in Oppland County, Norway. As she reminisces, "I started competing in cross-country when I was seven years old. When I was about 18 I started to think that I could have a long sporting career. I started to practice shooting more seriously, more than once a week. I wasn't very good at it before, but I got a lot better. I've also become a little bit stronger on the tracks too, which has increased my chances of success. All of a sudden I don't need to shoot clean all the time."[26] Often regarded as one of the fastest shooters on the range, from 2010-2012 she would regularly win individual World Cup races including World Championship gold in the individual and mass start events.[27] Her 2012/2013 season was one for the ages after winning 11 times on the World Cup circuit and sweeping all five individual crystal globes on offer.[2] Tora is currently 5th on the all-time World Cup victories list and has been involved with coaching the Norwegian junior girls team.

TWO SKIS AND A RIFLE: AN INTRODUCTION TO BIATHLON

Image 4.2. Tora Berger competing in the 7.5 km sprint race at the XXII Winter Olympic Games in Sochi, Russia. This would be her final appearance at the Olympics after her retirement in 2014. (Photo by Iurii Osadchi/Shutterstock.com)

It is difficult to recognize **Raphaël Poirée** in his new surroundings of the Bergen, Norway airport where he dons a construction hat and wears fluorescent yellow for his public works company job. Before the emergence of Martin Fourcade, Poirée was the greatest French biathlete of all time, and still takes 3rd spot on the all-time World Cup victories list with 44. And with eight World Championship titles and three medals at the 2002 and 2006 Olympics, Raphaël shed light on a sport with few followers at the time. From 1998-2007, he would claim four World Cup titles and win an individual discipline title on no fewer than 10 occasions.[28] Cursed to be competing in a time when Bjoerndalen was at his peak, Poirée had a very high 85.8% shooting accuracy and was only a marginally slower skier than Bjoerndalen. However, over the course of the 2003/2004 season, not even Bjoerndalen could nor would he ever match Poirée's complete sweep of the individual crystal globes.[29] After a final victory at the French Championships on April 1, 2007, Raphaël would hang up his skis and rifle to start a new chapter in life. He would later for a short period become the Belarusian men's coach in 2012 and now splits his time between Bergen and Eikelandsosen, Norway.[28]

On any given day, Belarusian **Darya Domracheva** was untouchable and skied with a languid and long striding technique that belied her brisk pace and was often seen passing rivals out of the shooting range or on steep uphill ascents. At the 2014 Sochi Winter Games, she was in dominating form and won three gold medals in the individual, pursuit, and mass start events. Such was Domracheva's form that her rivals were left thinking only about silver. "I thought she was going to win today, she was so strong in the last races I did not believe somebody could be faster than her," commented Gabriella Soukalova (now Koukalova), a multi-World Cup and overall points title winner. "I didn't race against her today; I thought it would be better to race with just myself."[30] In doing so, Domracheva became her countries most decorated Olympian in history. Later that same year, she would wrap up her finest season to date by winning the overall World Cup title. In a career that was wrought with difficulties including sickness, she missed the entire 2015/2016 season due to a bout with mononucleosis, Domracheva has nonetheless amassed 31 World Cup victories and surpassed both Berger and Disl for total number of wins during the 2017/2018 season.[2] From 2008 until after the 2010 Olympics, Darya filmed over 500 hours of footage highlighting in her own way the life of a biathlete which was pared down to a 50 minute film entitled, "Darya Domracheva: Representing Belarus."

TWO SKIS AND A RIFLE: AN INTRODUCTION TO BIATHLON

Image 4.3. Darya Domracheva competing at the 2014 Sochi Winter Olympic Games. (Photo by Lurii Osadchi/Shutterstock.com)

Seasoned professional **Johannes Thignes (JT) Boe** (NOR) and now retired **Kaisa Makarainen** (FIN) have solidified themselves as two of the greatest biathlon champions in history. While Kaisa announced her retirement for the second time at the conclusion of the 2019/2020 season, 31 year old JT Boe continues to find his stride as the dominant force in men's World Cup biathlon; a career which eventually will see him go down as one of the greatest of all time after now having won the overall title for the 5th time. He is often regarded as one of the fastest skiers the sport has ever seen and consistently betters the field by an unheard of 6%. Such is his prowess over the past few seasons in particular, where so far he has been victorious 85 times over 12 World Cup seasons and secured 8 Olympic medals (5 gold) from Pyeongchang and Beijing, he even was able to take time away from the

2nd trimester of competition during the 2019/2020 season to have a baby with his wife. Upon returning to the sport for the remainder of the season, where he is now considered the 3rd most successful male biathlete of all time, he picked up right where he left off; winning races and still capturing the overall World Cup title! JT Boe certainly hopes that his career will continue with the same longevity as Kaisa's did who after 16 seasons and some 431 World Cup starts amassed 3 World Cup overall titles, 6 individual discipline crystal globes, 85 World Cup podiums with 27 victories, and 5 World Championship medals. While the sport looks to JT Boe as the star, it has decided to continue on in the absence of "Queen Kaisa" whose endearing charm and perpetual smile will be greatly missed by her adoring fans.[34]

Chapter Five
Skiing: From Technology to Technique, it's Half the Battle

The word ski comes from old Norse "skid" meaning a split length or stick of wood. For many centuries in the snowy Scandinavian north, skis made from birch shaped into a sort of plank were strapped to boots and used for hunting game, gathering fire wood, and as a means to remain in social contact with friends in neighboring villages. Early skiers would use a single pole or stick to propel themselves forward or to slow down on descents by dragging the stick along the ground. Early advances in binding systems improved the contact between boot and ski and were based on the 19th century Fennoscandian model used in Drevja and Salla type skis. Known as the Kalvtrask ski, a thong was threaded vertically through holes and wrapped around the boot using badger skin in some cases to secure the boot in place. The indigenous Scandinavian Lapps on the contrary used a horizontal stem-hole binding system which is still used in present day skis.[1,2]

Norwegian military regiments organized skiing contests in the 18th century which would expand into the public sector in the mid-19th century with a race in Tromso on March 21, 1843. In 1892 the famous Holmenkollen ski festival would originate and subsequently go on to add a separate cross-country ski only race in 1901.[1,2] The diagonal stride was the "classic" technique of norm at the time which requires parallel grooves or tracks cut into the snow for the skis to follow. It is also an effective technique for making progress in deeper snow without pre-laid tracks. In classic skiing, a ski on one side (e.g., right) is weighted, pushed forward, and allowed to glide while the rearward leg (e.g., left) on the opposite side is moved naturally into a kick position.

For the next stride weight is then transferred to the other side (left) while the original ski (right) is used to push off from the snow, necessitating a means such as wax or grooved scales to grip the snow surface with the ski, following through into a kick finish. The opposite (left) leg is concurrently pushed into a gliding motion and the cycle repeats itself. Using poles adds propulsion and works in harmony with the classic stride where the arm opposite the leg in question follows suit, thus coining the term diagonal stride. Variants on the classic technique including the 'kick-double-pole', where one side kicks while both poles are planted adjacent to one another and thrust rearward, and double poling, both skis are allowed to glide in parallel with the only means of propulsion coming from simultaneously using both poles, are used on gently downhill to steeper descents.

One of the earliest advances in ski technology surfaced around the mid-19th century where Norwegian wood carvers added camber to the middle of the ski. Shaped like a bow, the camber arches up at the center of the ski directly beneath the boot to distribute the weight of the skier more evenly along the length of the ski. The camber design allowed the ski to be narrower from tip to tail yet without the nuisance of sinking into the snow. Additional benefits of this new design were that the ski floated over softer snow, absorbed bumps and other imperfections in the snow more readily, and was more maneuverable due to its lesser mass. Quality skis at this time were made of wood using ash or possibly even hickory imported from the United States which was tough to work with but produced a thin, flexible, and strong ski. A laminate ski, consisting of two layers of wood joined with glue, would appear at the turn of the century but proved unreliable as the glue would not indefinitely remain waterproof. The first attempt at making skis using an alternate material to wood is credited to Joseph Vicky of France who crafted skis out of solid aluminum. Ten years later, plastic, under the name Cellulix, was used for the first time as a base in French Dynamic skis and would eventually change the face of skiing forever.[3]

In subsequent years, fiberglass would be added to plastic skis as reinforcement, but early attempts by Bud Phillips Ski and Holley Ski using this new material would not endure long in the market. In 1959, the first all plastic downhill ski was invented by Fred Langendorf and Art Molnar in Montreal and from that point forward the concept proliferated reaching main stream popularity.[3] At the 1974 Nordic World Championships in Falun, Sweden, two Austrian ski companies, Fischer and Kneissl, debuted synthetic fiberglass cross-country skis.[4] First thought to be introduced in 1970 by John Lovett of Boulder, Colorado, a pair of fiberglass skis made by Kneissl were worn by Thomas Magnusson of Sweden on his way to victory in the 30 km World Championship event.[3,4] News of Magnusson's win spread like wildfire over the world's media and biathletes preparing for the Minsk Biathlon World Championships less than a week later would not be oblivious to this sensation. Champion biathletes at the time, like Alexander Tikhonov and Juhani Suutarinen, scrambled to lay their hands on fiberglass skis and other biathletes, after finishing a particular race, were even seen swiftly changing back to wood skis to appease sponsors. But the writing was on the wall and fiberglass signaled the death of wood skis and companies like Jarvinen who were either unwilling or incapable of adapting to this revolution.[4]

Nordic skiing technique out of necessity changed with the advances in ski technology. Compared to wood, fiberglass skis were much stiffer and required a more pronounced force or stomp to apply the kick wax, a sticky wax used on the ski base under the ball of the foot, which is used to drive the opposite ski into a gliding motion over the snow. With less interaction of the ski base underneath the foot and more so at the tip and tail of the ski, gliding became more important and diminished the reliance on the diagonal stride in favor of double poling. Increased gliding meant waxes underwent considerable advancement by Austrian design manufacturers who readily applied knowledge gained from alpine skiing to Nordic skis. As Seth Masia[5] writes, "because World Cup technicians don't share their secrets to success, much waxing lore has the apocryphal character of folktale." Nevertheless, advances in ski wax technology using surfactants and eventually fluorocarbons would be at the forefront of modern ski wax chemistry. A surfactant serves as a wetting agent, which normally goes against conventional thought for its use on skis; however, Terry Hertel in 1974 used sodium dodecyl sulfate (SDS) which, when suspended in paraffin wax, will clump into spheres with its hydrophobic (anti-water) side towards the snow. This created a sort of water-repellant ball bearing surface to the base of the ski and such was the speed of the wax that the apropos term "Super Hot Sauce" was coined to describe its effectiveness.[5] Other advances like carbon fiber ski poles and stiffer plastic boots and binding systems were ushered in to compliment fiberglass skis and ultimately led to the competition arrival of skating technique in the early 1980's.[4]

As early as the 1930's, alpine and cross-country skiers were using skating technique, which as the name implies is a style similar to ice skating, to travel across relatively flat terrain. Skating technique would prove very effective in the 1960's as a means of traversing over roads or flatter terrain during ski orienteering competitions. Pauli Siltonen was a particularly strong ski orienteer who eventually turned his attention to marathon cross-country ski races bringing with him an early form of skating, labeled marathon skating, where one leg would remain in a track while the other pushed off the snow at an angle. Others learned of Siltonen's technique and none would pursue this more thoroughly at the time than America's most accomplished Nordic skier Bill Koch.[6] After observing a competitor using skating technique on flat sections of a 30 km race in Sweden, Koch would ask himself why not apply this technique to sanctioned shorter distance races.[4] At the 1982 World Ski Championships held in Norway, Sweden's top Nordic skier Thomas Erikkson lost an incredible amount of time to Koch on a particular section of the course, where Koch had employed the marathon skating technique to win bronze at the event. At the conclusion of the season-long World Cup skiing competition, Koch using marathon skating would go on to win the overall title. Soon afterwards, Koch's competitors on the World Cup circuit would emulate his new marathon style, sometimes leaving a ski in a track but more commonly using both skis (double skating) in a technique known as V2 skate.[6]

Concern that this new technique would entirely supplant the diagonal stride began to promulgate within the International Ski Federation (FIS) in 1983 who would initially ban skating at the start and finish of races to shelter the spectators from seeing this 'corrupt' and non-traditional method. Since skating was allowed at all other points of the race, racers began to put glide wax on the entire length of their skis. The old Siltonen marathon approach had largely been abandoned in favor of having the gliding ski outside of the track, riding on the snow at a slight angle while the opposite ski was used for propulsion in a technique that came to be known as V1 skate.[6] Resistance to skating continued for the next couple of years; however, the persistence of ski manufacturers, who began producing skate only skis in volume, and top athletes forced the FIS to realize the technique was here to stay. By the time of the 1985 Nordic World Championships in Seefeld, Austria, all the top finishers had used skating, far distancing themselves from the nearest diagonal stride competitor. The FIS ultimately would decide that in order to preserve classic or diagonal stride technique as a feasible form of ski racing, separate races for skating vs. classic styles would need to be held. The UIPMB in a more sweeping move would decide on the lead-up to the 1988 Calgary Winter Games that biathletes would be allowed to utilize skating in all competitions.[4] Biathletes from Calgary onwards were now free to use this method at all World Cup, World Championship, and Olympic Games events and found skating technique more easily balanced the rifle on the back.

...

Modern biathletes like Finland's Kaisa Makarainen (image 5.1 below) predominantly employ one of three skating techniques, depending on the nature of the terrain, to navigate around ski loops. On steeper terrain, where the gradient can reach as much as 25%, biathletes employ the V1 (sometimes referred to as offset, G2, or 2nd gear) technique. With this technique, one side is generally dominant, but skilled athletes can readily switch from one side to the other depending on the direction of travel (e.g., if skiing around a right hand corner, the right side/leg is chosen as dominant and vice versa) or to reduce fatigue. When the ski (right side) makes contact with the snow at the beginning of the glide, the poles, which according to the IBU may be no longer than the height of the athlete[7], are planted simultaneously in front of the skier. Normally, the pole on the gliding side (right) will be planted in a slightly more vertical manner than the opposite side which must accommodate for the angle of the opposite ski. As the glide commences, both poles, which are held in place on the wrist via thinly padded straps, are thrust backward into full arm extension to propel the body forward, finishing with relaxed hands. An athletic stance is called upon to shift one's body weight to the opposite (left) side, and as that ski glides the arms are flexed back towards the front of the body. Weight is once again shifted to the opposite (right) side for the sequence to continue in totality what can be described as a 1 (pole & step):2 (glide):3 (skate push opposite side) cadence. Dependence on the poles during V1 is relatively important compared to other skating techniques, contributing to as much as or more than 50% of power towards forward propulsion on uphill sections of a course.

Image 5.1. Kaisa Makarainen using V1 technique to ascend steeper terrain in Tyumen, Russia. (Photo by Valeri Potapova/ Shutterstock.com)

More efficient and by far the most commonly used yet difficult skating technique to master during biathlon competition is the V2 (one skate, G3, or 3rd gear) method. Top skiers like Makarainen or Denise Herrmann (GER) can gain as much as 5-6% time (or 1:30 seconds in a race lasting 25 minutes) over the field using in part the V2 skate because of better technique, natural talent or higher fitness; the latter of which serves to prolong time spent in V2 and delays the transition back to slower V1 as the terrain dictates. The primary difference in V2 compared to V1 technique is that with every weight transfer onto a ski, the poles will also be planted, instead of every other time as in V1. When observing an athlete from the front, imagine that the hips trace a "U" shaped pattern during weight transfer from one ski to the other. As the skier returns a ski into contact with the snow, he/she would be in an erect position with the arms extended forward and poles already planted. Once the glide commences, the knee on the gliding ski is bent, dropping the hip downward, while the poles are thrust rearward. The arms then swing the poles back to the front, poles are planted, and then weight is shifted to the opposite side ski forming the bottom and opposite top of the "U" as the hip slides across and then up to facilitate an erect posture. The bent knee and rearward pole thrust sequence on the opposite side occurs in an overall 1 (pole):2 (step):3 (glide) respective side cadence of V2 skating as biathletes race alone or in clusters around the course. The same cadence would continue on the opposite side as weight is transferred from right to left and then back again. Contemporary thought dictates that a shorter stride (faster cadence or ski cycle rate) is more proficient, yet distinguished skiers like Darya Domracheva placed greater emphasize on glide over cadence by employing a longer stride. The jury remains in deliberation on the economy of stride length, but in watching the field of World Cup biathletes race, the keen observer will discern a variety of subtly personalized yet masterfully effective styles.

Image 5.2. Laura Dahlmeier mid-stride in V2 (or possibly V2 alternate) technique during the World Cup sprint race, Nove Mesto, 2015. (Photo by Petr Toman/Shutterstock.com)

When speeds start to increase beyond what would be effective for V2, V2 alternate (two skate, G4, or 4th gear) is utilized to increase glide and distance covered while poling thus making wax choice a very important proposition. In what might appear to be a similar technique to V1 where poling only occurs on one side, the timing for propulsion is actually the same for V2 alternate as it is in V2. A similar compression of the body at the hip and knee occurs on the gliding ski; however, unlike V2 the skier in V2 alternate remains in a lower position for the duration of the glide. Skiers use V2 poling on the gliding ski, but the real advantage comes on the non-poling side where the arms remain behind the athlete as they ride the ski in a low position. From this bent position, the arms swing aggressively forward as the skier performs a skate push to return to the poling side ski.[8] The synchronization of the swinging arms and skate push generates considerable speed and athletes like Martin Fourcade often approach or even exceed 30 km/h (18 mph) using this technique.[9]

On steeper downhills, when skating becomes impossible, biathletes will assume an aerodynamic full tuck position similar to alpine downhill skiers while following parallel tracks that are often cut into the course. Not all downhill sections on a course will contain tracks and without metal edges as is the case on modern skate skis, navigating icy corners at high speed can be tricky at best. It is not uncommon to observe biathletes or cross-country skiers falling near the bottom of a descent while trying to navigate a bend in the course utilizing step turns; a technique that maintains glide while deliberately lifting and redirecting skis one at a time into the turn. Once the course begins to level out following a downhill section, biathletes will be seen transitioning from a tuck to V2 alternate and then V2 and/or V1 as necessary. Approaching the finish line on flat terrain, biathletes will disregard using their poles altogether and 'free skate' (G5), similar in approach to ice skating, to the line which proves very fast yet exhausting and can only be maintained for short bursts. A final thrust of the leg across the line breaks the timing light and to the obvious relief of many a biathlete, who over a season average anywhere from 26-27 km/h (16.5 mph; men) and 23-24 km/h (14.5 mph; women), the skiing for the day is concluded.[9]

...

Ski technology advancements continued into the 1970's with prepreg fiberglass, a term for fabric reinforcement with pre-impregnated resins made from fiberglass, S-glass which is a chemically altered fiberglass material, and mixing of fiberglass with other materials such as Kevlar, carbon fiber, and ceramic fiber. Little detailed information exists on

TWO SKIS AND A RIFLE: AN INTRODUCTION TO BIATHLON

the exact manufacturing process of today's World Cup skis but certain characteristics are common between brands. Considerations for companies marketing skis to world class athletes include the core construction, which may resemble a honeycomb structure similar to that used for aeronautical engineering projects such as the space shuttle; such are the time, energy, and resources gone into the technology. A tapered design, when observing the ski from the side, from tip, to middle, and then again to the tail further reduces weight and optimizes flexibility of the ski during skating. Carbon fiber laminates, proprietary sidewalls to assist skiers with glide, steering and power transmission, slight tapered designs (viewing the ski from top), and proprietary side cuts add to the complexity of a modern ski. On any given race day, top biathletes will have several pairs of skis to select from ranging in length (minimum is limited to the height of the biathlete minus four cm), grind (see waxing discussion in this chapter), wax type, and stiffness (soft, medium, and stiff) depending on the course and/or snow conditions.

All the technology that goes into ski manufacturing would be pointless if not for the ability to interface the racer to the ski. Until the mid-2000's, bindings were drilled onto the ski after carefully determining the best location for the skier above the ski camber. The primary disadvantage of this method of mounting the binding was that changes in the field were impossible; the mounting location had to be redrilled. In a joint effort by several companies, the Nordic Integrated System (NIS) was introduced in 2005 to be compatible with New Nordic Norm (NNN) binding systems, which employs a bar in the toe of a skate boot that is secured onto a latch or catch on the binding. The advantage of the NIS system is that a plate is drilled onto the ski to which the NNN binding is secured, allowing modulation fore and aft in the field.[10] Skate ski boots are manufactured with the NNN bar installed and along with other technological advances, like use of a carbon fiber chassis to maximize stiffness and light weight, breathable waterproofing, Velcro enclosures to compliment micro-adjustable buckles, a rigid sole that mates to the NNN binding, and forward canting hinge design to facilitate slight ankle flexion marries the interface of boot/binding to ski. Advancements to the NIS and NNN systems never cease as several companies have developed bindings that enhance a skiers 'feel' on the snow or allow skiers the ability to adjust the position of the binding without need for removing skis, potentially enabling on-the-fly adjustments as conditions dictate (more relevant to classic skis).

Base material also improved in the 1970's concurrent with ski technology after the advent of sintered polyethylene which proves to be faster, stronger, and more wax retentive than ever before.[3] Often referred to as P-Tex, which is actually a brand name for base material coined by International Mountain Sports, the surface of the ski in contact with snow or base is made of ultra-high molecular weight polyethylene (UHMW). Ski bases are closely related to the material used to create opaque milk jugs, containing polyethylene molecules (C_2H_4) linked together in long chains. When the polyethylene molecules reach a particular molecular weight, it is capable of being sintered, which allows the material to be molded without melting. Manufacturers like Fischer, Atomic, Madshus, and Rossignol press the powder form of polyethylene together, which forces the molecules into chains. After the polyethylene has been molded or sintered, the bases themselves are created in one of two ways, continuous compression molding (CCM) or scything.[11]

In CCM, two titanium belts are set apart and in close proximity to one another. As polyethylene powder is fed between the two belts, the molecules are compressed and as a result heated to upwards of 500°F (260°C), creating a ribbon of usable base material. Scything on the other hand uses a large press that forms a large round block or cake of material called a billet. Powder is sifted down into a cavity prior to the press compressing the material. As the material is pressed, the temperature, like CCM, is raised which creates a solid material that can be sliced or scythed into ribbons. Sintered bases, due to the nature of the polyethylene bonding, crucially contain 'pores' which allow excellent surface wax adherence, increasing speed over the snow surface for longer periods of time. Additives to the polyethylene molecules such as graphite help to reduce static electricity buildup and create the self-lubricating black surface of modern skate skis. Other materials such as fluorocarbon powders or Gallium were added to the mix following a recipe held secret by top Nordic ski manufacturers.[11,12]

...

Terry Hertel, of "Super Hot Sauce" wax infamy, would eventually talk with 3M chemist Rob Hunter in the mid-1980's about something that would work in wet and dirty spring snow to keep skis fast. Hunter mentioned the company sold a liquid fluorocarbon ("fluor" in short) that dried to a smooth and glossy finish, but at $1,000 per pound, its application in the ski industry was questionable. Hertel would buy the liquid in large drums and to it added a high strength wax, creating a block that he called Racing 739 which would become the first marketed fluorocarbon wax. Over at the Swix wax company, chief chemist Leif Torgersen was looking for his own wax to repel dirt and he found it in Italy at the Enichem SpA industrial company who had a fluorocarbon powder that would melt at about 155°C (311°F). That exceeds the melting temperature of a sintered base but if carefully applied with an iron that was kept moving, the wax would melt into the base without damaging the base material. The company would introduce their fluorocarbon wax commercially in 1990 as Cera F.[5]

The noteworthiness of the advent of fluorocarbon wax cannot be understated and historically must be considered one of the single greatest advances in Nordic ski technology. Several companies jumped at the opportunity to supply elite Nordic and biathlon teams with numerous fluorocarbon wax cocktails to maximize glide when confronted with a myriad of environmental conditions.

The race day starts early for wax technicians who arrive to the stadium and head out on course to begin a series of mini experiments, to determine snow and atmospheric conditions. An athlete can have perfect shooting but without 'good' skis, there is very little chance of winning or even reaching the podium. Preparing skis can be broken down into three steps, the paraffin, powder, and structure or grind. Depending on the conditions of the day, all three are manipulated to find the best possible scenario of wax and grind. Rarely do teams share their strategies with the competition so ski preparation becomes a sort of competition within the competition. Head technicians, like Danielo Muller of Team Belarus, will carry a thermometer and hygrometer to measure skiing conditions including the temperature of the snow and air/water content (humidity) in the snow, respectively.[13] Other snow characteristics such as size and shape of crystals and dirt content can be inferred from prevailing conditions. For example, a recent snowfall can produce conditions that range from dry, windblown, glazed, damp, or saturated snow while man-made snow will exhibit slightly different characteristics such as being hard, packed, moist, 'sugar', and/or saturated. Whichever characteristics predominate on the day dictate in part wax and/or ski choice and is as much an art as it is science.[12]

When the temperature of the snow is very low, the crystals become very sharp and inelastic which tend to bite into the wax on the base of the ski, hindering glide and increasing wax wear. Therefore, a harder wax applied to a smooth base is preferable when such conditions are present. Cold to medium temperature snow does not bite into the wax nearly as much as extremely cold snow, offers less friction, and allows a wider variety of softer waxes to be applied to the base. As the snow approaches the freezing mark, a new set of challenges occur where high amounts of water create a 'suction' effect and increased potential for icing. Fluorocarbons seemed to be best in these conditions because of their tendency to reduce surface tension and increase glide. A special consideration is made when the course has been groomed into 'corduroy' which artificially ages the snow, rounds snow crystals, and increases the likelihood that softer waxes will prove more effective.[12]

What wax technicians are searching for in a wax necessitates an understanding of how skis are thought to glide over the surface of the snow. As Nat Brown explains, if the amount of friction between the ski and snow is controlled and just the right amount of snow is melted, a thin layer of water is created for the skis to slide over. By selecting the perfect wax hardness for the day's snow conditions, snow crystals will bite into the wax layer, generating enough friction to melt a fine layer of snow. Wax technicians must consider the shape of the snow crystal, temperature of the snow, snow strength, and saturation level when determining the best wax on the day. A wax that is too hard will not melt snow because of a lack of friction, while too soft a wax will melt more snow than necessary and produce suction which reduces glide. Brown continues to explain that surface tension, which is a function of the size and shape of water droplets formed beneath the base of the ski, can be controlled with the proper wax. Large water droplets are thought to produce suction, while smaller round droplets create a ball-bearing like effect between the base and snow. Fluorocarbon waxes, as opposed to paraffins (traditional wax much like that of a candle), created higher surface tensions and lower friction which resulted in smaller beads of water beneath the ski base.[12] Despite such overwhelming reliance on fluorinated ski waxes, a move by the

International Ski Federation or FIS to ban its use because of detrimental health and environmental concerns eventually worked its way into the biathlon world and in 2020, the IBU committed to banning the use of fluorocarbon waxes, technically "C8 fluorocarbon" (or perfluorooctanoic acid) in the near future. On March 22, 2023, that move became official and its use for ski preparation has been officially banned posing new challenges for waxing technicians for all national teams.[16,17] In turn, radical changes were in order as U.S. Team Manager Fede Fontana explained including completely new fluor free equipment and tools like brushes, cleaning of ski bags and switching the focus to other areas of ski preparation like grinding and hand structuring. Teams in the meantime will utilize non-fluor waxes from leading companies and wait for the next magic substance to come out which may take several years to realize.[18] Other factors such as dry lubrication, additives, and dirt repellence all will influence glide and the perfect combination of wax choice is the prize that all wax technicians hunt for in each race.

Once all environmental factors have been considered, it's off to a well-ventilated wax truck or cabin where a team of technicians from each nation preps skis with suggested waxes and base structures. Plural here because top biathletes may travel with twenty pairs of skis, selecting up to eight pairs on race day from several wax combinations, structures, and flexes; soft, medium, or hard flex on a ski is determined at the camber with an athlete's full (FBW) or half (HBW) body weight. The closer the camber is to the surface of the snow while being weighted (e.g., 1.1 mm for FBW, 2.6 mm for HBW) the less stiff the ski and vice versa. Optimally, skis will make uniform contact along the length of the ski, which interestingly can change with the atmospheric temperature; many warm skis counterintuitively are stiffer than a cold ski and have less contact with snow along the length of the base structure.[14] Much is depending on the five or so technicians to properly prepare the skis each of whom has a specific role in creating the finished product.

Image 5.3. Norwegian technicians preparing skis for competition at the 2017 IBU World Championships, Hochfilzen, Austria. (Photo by Anrephoto/Shutterstock.com)

The initial step is to remove old wax using a scraper which takes the base down to its raw P-Tex material. Several methods are employed to smooth the surface as even new skis direct from the factory may have imperfections. A steel scraper, sanding, or stone grinding, which is an art form unto itself as teams often send skis out periodically to a particular artisan for grinding, serve to 'open' the base to more readily accept wax. Skis are then rilled or pressed with a machine, sometimes hand held, to provide a pattern or structure that helps reduce suction particularly in warmer conditions. With information in hand from the earlier snow and atmospheric mini experiments, the skis are now ready for wax. A technician may crayon or drip melted carbon, paraffin, or other secret ingredient wax onto the base using a specially modified iron that closely resembles what, if you are at all like me, might be collecting dust in your laundry room. The iron is then run along the base of the ski in the direction of travel, spreading the wax evenly into the pores. After the wax has cooled, it is scraped to a thin layer with a plastic scraper and then brushed by hand or with an electric rotary tool using horsehair or nylon to polish the wax to a very smooth sheen. A powder is sprinkled onto the base, and then either ironed or literally 'corked' in by running a block of cork along the base to slightly melt the wax to the wax sublayer beneath.[12,13] A final brushing using felt polishes the expensive wax (40 grams of powder or other wax may retail for over 100 dollars!) to a thin membrane and the skis are now ready for testing by biathletes and wax technicians, many of whom are outstanding skiers in their own right.

Testing of ski conditions continues until just before the race, and ski choice becomes a collective decision between the head wax technician and the biathlete. Athletes and technicians are allowed on the course, wearing their official bibs, within three hours prior to the race and many teams will utilize a number of approaches to testing wax and skis. Electronic speed traps determine the speed of a racer between two fixed points and in theory a pair of skis used by the same racer that travels the distance in a shorter period of time has better glide. The simplest test is to start at a common point at the top of a slight descent and simply glide until the skis come to a rest. The farther the distance traveled, the better the glide.[12,13] But it may come down to the biathlete's or technician's subjective feel, simply a sensation conveyed to the brain that 'xyz' ski is faster. Switching from one pair of skis to another with slightly different waxes or structures will often result in one pair of skis performing noticeably better. In fact, as Nat Brown[12] describes when using a subjective feel approach to prepare skis for an athlete, "good skiers can compare skis very accurately. I once had Bill Koch [silver medalist at the 1976 Winter Olympics] rate six pairs this way. I had just tested the same skis through the speed traps, and Bill was able to rank them exactly the same way I had done with my instruments."

While the wax technicians are communicating with one another via 2-way radio from out on the course to the wax cabin (technicians are allowed to continue ski tests until five minutes prior to the race) the athletes are preparing in their own way for the race. Race day TV coverage shows the athletes having their clothing and rifles inspected and if found not in compliance, correcting the infraction, whether because of too little trigger weight (see Chapter Six) or improper advertising size or location (e.g., national emblems on a biathlete's hat must be no larger than 3 cm^2), must transpire before he/she is allowed on the race starting line. Forty-five minutes prior to the start of competition, several fluor test stations open to allow teams to have their skis tested for this now banned substance. After a sticker is placed on skis indicating the athlete in question, a Bruker Alpha II device (a machine that passes infrared radiation over a compound and checks for unique absorption profiles) scans skis at 3 points for fluor. If found to be in the 'green zone', skis are well below the threshold for fluor containing wax and are ready for competition. Similar to soccer or 'futbol' rules, yellow and red cards are issued to teams if higher levels of fluor are detected.[19] Skis are again checked for fluor after the race and also for proper length (no less than 10 cm below skiers height), weight (minimum 750 grams minus bindings), and other properties as determined by an IBU official.[7] Temperature primarily dictates clothing selection but athletes tend to err on the side of being cold at the start knowing very well that as the race progresses their core temperatures will rise. From warm temperatures where athletes may cut out sleeves on their long-sleeved, one-piece, and seamless racing suit to frigid days where balaclavas, neck warmers/scarves, racing hats, heavier gloves over a liner with a trap door for the trigger finger, chemical hand warmers, technical undergarments, adhesive patches on the nose and cheeks, and goggles that can be flipped up to sight the target when shooting are the norm, it is clear that clothing choice is critical. As the race continues to draw near, all biathletes are fitted with red transponders strapped to each ankle to electronically start/stop the race timer, which is why at the finish of many a race fans will notice a skier often thrusting her/his leg across the line to stop the clock.

Image 5.4. IBU official readying transponders for World Cup biathletes. (Photo by Petr Toman/Shutterstock.com)

Minutes before the race, biathletes will jog in their race boots while listening to their favorite music through headphones or perform calisthenic type exercises in the staging area adjacent to the starting grid while removing layers of clothing as their body temperatures rise. A final choice of ski structure and wax combinations from the prepared

TWO SKIS AND A RIFLE: AN INTRODUCTION TO BIATHLON

skis are made in some cases moments before the start, truly making this a team effort where trust and experience are paramount. Head wax technicians often keep a journal of ski preparations made over the years and rely on prior observations when conditions are fickle and anticipated to change from say man-made snow to fresh powder as the race develops. Technicians and coaches will choose in this case between the better combination of wax and structure for either the early or later stages of the race. Get it all right, and the wax technician is a hero for the day. At about 2-3 minutes before the start, biathletes will grab their skis and carbon fiber poles with their high strength to weight ratio, and walk or jog to their grid position confirmed by their bib number. While trying to keep pre-race nerves in check, on cold days when the temperature drops hands start to lose circulation, partly because gloves tend to err on the side of tactility rather than warmth, many an athlete will be seen performing arm windmill exercises at the start or when entering the shooting range to restore blood flow to their extremities.

Out on course now, whether or not the right ski selection was made will be ever apparent to the biathlete who will often give credit to a wax technician at post-race interviews. "My wax crew did an excellent job today and definitely gave me an advantage. I was gliding past everyone on the downhills so I was able to pick up a few places just from having the fast skis" commented Clare Egan, U.S. National Team biathlete after a particular 10 km pursuit race.[15] Faster skiers yell "track!" as they approach slower competitors on the course who are obligated to get out of the way so that the faster skier gains the best line around corners or remains in the best snow. A missed shot results in a penalty loop for most competition formats, but watch out, those already on the loop have the right of way to return to the race course as athletes crisscross into and out of the loop. On not so rare occasions, a pole will snap if placed too close to another competitor's ski or if planted in between the V stride of their own ski, a common rookie mistake that even top pros occasionally make. Competitors may exchange poles or even a broken ski, should a binding or ski itself fail, and each nation will strategically place staff around the course with spare skis, poles, and even beverages on hand just in case a need arises. However, skis cannot be changed nor is any substance allowed to be applied in attempt to improve glide so once the ski choice has been made before the race, competitors finish on those same skis. After a final debriefing on ski performance following the race, athletes focus on their recovery nutrition, may receive a massage, and rest to begin preparations for the next race.

Chapter Six
Going Clean

The best biathlon skiers in the world, the top 5% of all competitors, might be capable of making up lost time after a missed shot or two at most, but for the vast majority it signals a deficit that likely will see a podium placing vanish in a flash. With a fortitude and steadfastness for competition, it's amazing to watch an athlete who knows after missing several shots that a top finish is impossible against the world's best, yet they continue to race with an incomparable grit to the finish. Persevering through a difficult shooting bout, or even stretches of lackluster performance, are what separate champions from the rest of the field as a biathlete looks forward to better execution in the next race. What every biathlete is striving for is that consistency of position, timing, and feeling of being in control when the pressure of leading a race or fighting for position is on the line. Years of training and shooting tens of thousands of practice rounds a year are a must and the norm to be successful and reach the elusive 90% accuracy or even better in some cases over the course of a World Cup season. Perhaps needless to say, the rifle becomes an extension of a biathlete's being, a third arm if you will, after repeatedly stripping and cleaning their rifle week after week, memorizing every slide, spring, nut, blemish, and bolt.

Following the transition to the small bore .22 LR rifle in 1978, few manufacturers have made a greater impact on the sport than Anschütz. Founded in 1856 by Julius Gottfried Anschütz, son of Johann Heinrich Gottlieb, the company initially produced pocket pistols and shotguns in Zella-Mehlis, Germany. Over the years, Anschütz has had great success at international shooting contests, World Championships, and the Olympics.[1] The vast majority of biathletes use an individually customized Anschütz rifle; however, it is not uncommon to see Russian or other former Soviet state biathletes using Izhmash rifles manufactured by Kalashnikov Concern, the largest arms manufacturer in Russia headquartered in Udmurtia and Moscow. Whichever manufacturer an athlete chooses, or more likely receives sponsorship from, there are similar characteristics shared between rifles. Image 6.1 below provides a reference for the reader on the major parts of a generic biathlon rifle.

Image 6.1. The Anschütz Model 1827 F Biathlon rifle provides World Cup competitors a platform for customizing their own rifle. Many top biathletes will scrap the stock in favor of a custom piece made to their specifications. Note the magazine clips stored in the forestock with one inserted in the feeder ahead of the trigger. The release lever for the magazine is just ahead of the trigger and behind the inserted magazine. The bolt handle just above the trigger slides the straight pull action rearwards. (Photo courtesy of J.G. Anschütz GmbH & Co. KG)

Martin Fourcade (image 6.2) is seen holding his heavily modified biathlon rifle in preparation for a standing shoot. Starting at the front of the rifle, farthest from the athlete, a sight containing a snow cover is clamped to the barrel and may be adjusted for height above the barrel. The front or fore sight is a cylinder itself, containing a slot for an insert or aperture and when viewed from behind (looking into the cylinder) creates the appearance of two concentric circles formed by the round sight and aperture within. After shooting biathletes will often be seen flipping the snow cover closed, which is hinged on one side, to prevent snow falling from above (it is winter after all) or following a fall out on course from entering the sight to prevent blocking of the sight picture. Once they glide into the range, the snow cover is normally flipped open in order to view the target through the site but it's not unheard of to see athletes getting into their position, sighting the target, only to then realize that they forgot to flip open the cover; a break in the normal routine. As such, on sunny days, many will simply leave the cover open for the duration of the race. Continuing to work back on the rifle from the front site, the barrel is 550 mm long, precision manufactured, and bored internally (spirals cut or pressed inside the barrel which imparts a spin on the bullet) to maximize shooting performance.[1] Such is the accuracy that if the rifle were to be locked in place and fired at a paper target 50 meters away, the variation in spread of the bullet would be minimal giving the appearance of each bullet passing through the previous bullet's hole. On occasion biathletes will clamp a cylindrical weight to the front of the barrel behind the site in attempt to stabilize the rifle in windy conditions. At the rear of the barrel, closest to the athletes, is the action or 'barreled action'. Collectively, the barreled action includes the firing chamber and pin, straight pull action, and magazine/bullet feeder onto which the trigger assembly is attached.

Image 6.2. Martin Fourcade preparing to fire his rifle during a standing shoot in Tyumen, Russia. (Photo by Valeri Potapova/Shutterstock.com)

In the early 1980's, Peter Fortner, a gunsmith from Rohrdorf, Germany, agreed to rebuild an old bolt action biathlon rifle to improve the athletes speed from one shot to the next. Previous versions needed shooters to remove their hands from the pistol grip in order to feed another bullet into the firing chamber, so Fortner developed a straight pull action that only required use of the index finger and thumb to expel a spent cartridge and load a new bullet. What became known as the 'Fortner bolt action' revolutionized the sport of biathlon and is used in 95% of rifles on the World Cup circuit.[2] The rifle now remains steady with minimal movements needed to load and reload bullets between each shot, so biathletes can remain locked into a particular prone or standing position for all five shots at the range. Working in tandem with the straight pull action are the red and black magazines

TWO SKIS AND A RIFLE: AN INTRODUCTION TO BIATHLON

each containing five .22 caliber bullets which biathletes must remove (when empty of bullets after the previous shooting) and reload into the feeder at the range prior to each shooting. On rare occasion, a bullet cartridge may jam in the magazine or firing chamber, forcing the biathlete to reload by hand a spare single bullet into the firing chamber from above instead of automatically being fed from beneath. With each index finger pull of the straight pull lever on the side of the rifle, which is in many cases customized by the biathlete, a spent bullet case is expelled. The thumb then pushes the breech forward locking a new bullet cartridge fed by the magazine into the chamber, which is now ready to be fired at the target.

The trigger is a masterpiece of construction and may be fine-tuned by an athlete in several ways. The trigger blade, which must be surrounded by a rigid guard to prevent unwanted firing, contains a rough or knurled texture to enhance feel, particularly on cold days when fingers lose circulation. The blade itself can be moved up or down and rotated along its axis by a biathlete to find the best interface between the index finger and trigger blade. Most biathletes will employ a two-stage trigger where the first stage moves the trigger with minimal resistance to the firing point, essentially taking up the slack on the trigger to get a feel for its movement. At the end range of the first stage trigger movement, the biathlete will encounter a slight resistance to any further movement of the trigger, sometimes called the trigger point. Further pulling of the trigger with the index finger from this point will lead to the rifle firing and is known as the second stage. The trigger is adjustable for weight, in that the force required to overcome the resistance of firing a bullet or the trigger point may be modulated but must be at least 0.5 kg or slightly over one pound of force.[1,3] Movement of the trigger beyond the trigger point, or point of firing, is considered the sear engagement and the optimal feeling of overcoming the sear has been described as breaking glass in a quick snap.

Sitting atop the very rear of the barreled action is the rear or aft sight that works in tandem with the front/fore sight to visualize the biathlon target located 50 meters away. Unlike the front sight which is clamped around the barrel, the rear sight is slid along two grooves and then clamped to the rifle, allowing fore and aft adjustments to suit the shooter's eye. A block, or riser plate may also be attached beneath the rear sight to raise it as necessary for better alignment with the front sight. The rear sight contains a housing and cylinder or tube, which reduces unwanted light or glare from entering into the sight, as well as a snow cover at the front which serves the same purpose as the front sight. When looking at the sight from the rear, it appears to resemble a disc or cone with a small pinhole at its center. The biathlete will look through this pinhole towards the front sight and into the aperture to line up the biathlon target in what resembles a series of progressively smaller concentric circles. The image (6.3) below illustrates the ideal appearance of the biathlete's sight picture including the largest rear sight circle or ring, followed by the front sight ring, the aperture within, and finally the circular biathlon target at center. Notice that each progressively smaller ring is centered within the larger surrounding ring, which indicates that the rifle is aimed as close as possible to the center of the biathlon target. In attempt to further reduce light or unwanted movements noticed by peripheral vision many biathletes will attach a rectangular blinder to the rear sight which wraps around one or both eyes. Contemporary thought dictates that both eyes should remain open during shooting to reduce fatigue and allow a more natural vision when sighting the target and the blinder aids in this process.[4] Once the rifle has been fired, the .22 caliber bullet travels rapidly towards the target at a velocity approaching, but not exceeding, according to IBU rules, 360 meters per second or equivalent to 1,180 feet per second.[3]

TWO SKIS AND A RIFLE: AN INTRODUCTION TO BIATHLON

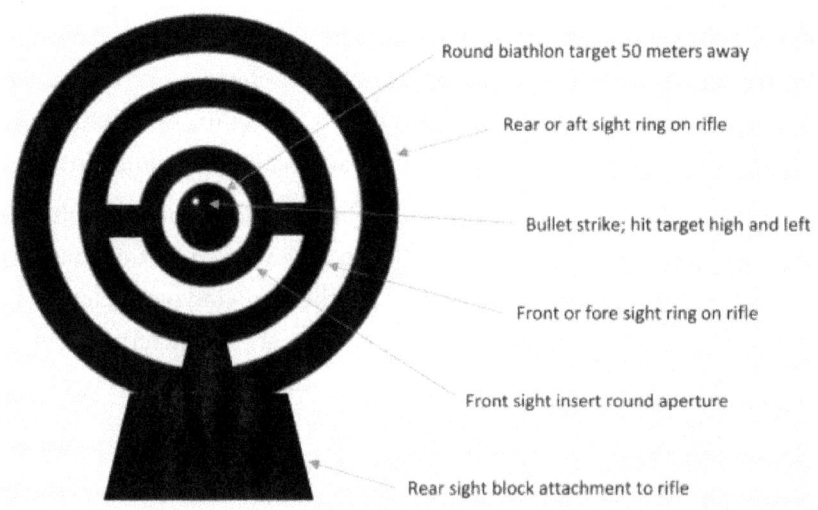

Image 6.3. Sight picture of a biathlete aiming at a biathlon target. The bullet strike is shown for illustrative purposes and in actuality would be visible only for a brief moment, just long enough for coaches and/or biathletes to visualize the strike, prior to a white plate covering the target after a successful shot. (From author's personal archive)

On windy days, rather than the biathlete trying to compensate by aiming left/right or high/low of the target, he/she will use sight adjustment knobs located on the side or top of the rear sight housing. To assist a biathlete with making real-time adjustments, wind flags made of light nylon that rotate 360 degrees are placed in the ground at five and thirty meters distance between the biathlete and the target on the shooting range.[3] If a flag is blowing to the left, the biathlete will realize that the bullet will be pushed in the same direction, and so the rear sight is adjusted using a knob on the side of the housing to effectively move the aiming point slightly to the right. In a sense, the rear sight is adjusted so that the target remains in the middle of the sight picture but aims the rifle to the right, tricking the biathlete into shooting to the right to compensate for the wind. The same principle is used for wind coming from behind or the front, where the knob on top of the rear sight housing changes the elevation of the bullet. Wind from behind tends to push a bullet up (lessening of the parabolic flight pattern of a bullet over a distance) whereas wind coming into the biathlete will push the bullet down.[4] Turning the elevation knob one way or the other will cause the bullet to be aimed higher or lower as necessary and each click of the knob, whether for windage or elevation, redirects a bullet approximately two mm at 50 meters distance. Biathletes through experience will guestimate wind strength by referencing the wind flags, using fewer clicks on light wind days or several clicks when the flag is fully flapping in the breeze.

The most customized part of a biathlete's rifle is the stock/butt assembly (technically the forestock from just behind the trigger guard forward is separate from the butt; however, both are combined into a single modular piece on modern rifles) which an athlete may use all season long during competition and for training in the 'off' season.[6] Stocks are generally made from shaped wood onto which a carbon fiber overlay is applied to best optimize the individual ergonomics of the biathlete.[5] When customizing a stock, consideration is given to how the position and relationship of the right (or left as it may be; discussion here assumes right handed shooter) hand and trigger finger conform to the pistol grip of the rifle. A notch behind the trigger well positions the thumb in a somewhat vertical position and increases stability with each shot. The left hand will need to be stable yet in a comfortable position during both prone and standing shooting. As such, finger grooves and a grip for the left hand, normally in the position of the "forend raiser block", provide a stable platform for holding the rifle while standing.[1] The flat-bottomed forestock becomes the platform for the left hand to grip in the prone position.[6] At the rear and top of the stock near the butt is an adjustable cheek piece that may move fore/aft, laterally, and up/down to align the head/eye with the sights on the rifle.

To further assist a biathlete's stability in the prone position, a cuff worn around the upper left arm containing a D-ring connects a sling and bungee corded hook system that is at its front attached to a track on the bottom of the forestock towards the mid-point of the barrel. The sling may be moved forward or back in the track to adjust the hand stop position for bracing the left hand. Collectively, the arm cuff, sling, and hand stop work in tandem to secure the rifle in the shoulder and provide a stable platform for the left arm. A customized metal and rubber padded buttplate at the very rear of the rifle stock is used to brace the rifle against the anterior (front) part of the shoulder. Buttplates employ a hook at the top to rest against the superior (top) aspect of the shoulder, and may be adjusted up/down, in (towards the stock) or out, and laterally as necessary to optimize the position of biathlete; especially the eye to sight relationship. With so many features to consider when fitting a stock, biathletes often will send measurements to a craftsman who after some 50 hours of handwork creates a one-off design specifically made for their body dimensions and preferred rifle positions. Even then, competitors will often tinker in the spring time, after the season ends and before training starts, with stocks or shooting positions from year to year in the hope of finding a permanent solution.[6,12]

Rounding out the anatomy of a biathlon rifle, a carrying harness is attached along the left side of the stock. Towards the end of the forestock, a small rod is bolted into the wood/carbon fiber material to which padded shoulder straps, much resembling those used on a small back pack, run for several inches ending at bungee cords which are then attached by a plate or are threaded through hollow or solid butt stocks, allowing positional adjustments. The biathlete uses the carrying harness to travel with the rifle while skiing around the course, slipping into and out of the harness as necessary when exiting and entering the shooting range. The stock also contains receptacles, at positions customized by many biathletes, for magazines which are magnetized to hold the five bullet magazines securely in place.[5] Extra bullets may individually be placed into small holes on the rifle and are used in relay events in particular. Bullets themselves each weigh about 40 grains (2.59 grams or about the weight of a penny) and have a flat projectile surface at front to maximize accuracy and a mild lubrication helps to quickly chamber the bullet in low temperatures.[7] All told, a biathlon rifle and all accessories, minus magazines and ammunition, is quite light but must weigh no less than 7.7 pounds (3.5 kg) according to IBU rules.[3]

...

Prior to any race, biathletes are given the opportunity to make sure their rifle is firing accurately in a process known as 'zeroing'. Carrying rifles to the range in soft cases containing a clear window to display the straight pull action, athletes are given a 45 minute window to shoot their rifles at paper targets placed at the same level and distance as the competition metal targets. Lane preference (there are thirty lanes at any given biathlon shooting range) is given to national federations with more competitors and highly ranked biathletes. The shooting range is centrally located in the stadium area to maximize visibility for spectators who rambunctiously cheer on their national heroes. Considerable precautions are taken to ensure that the range is safe through utilization of concrete or earthen banking on all sides to avoid ricocheted bullets from straying too far. At the Holmenkollen course in Oslo, part of the race track actually lies just above the shooting range and bullet proof glass(!) is employed to protect skiers on course while others are shooting. At 50 meters distance from the firing line is a row of metal biathlon targets, one for each shooting lane. When skiing into the range from the shooter's position/view, biathletes enter from the left and proceed to shoot either in the prone or standing position. Shooting lanes, each approximately three meters wide, are divided in half with the right side (lanes 1-15) for shooting in the prone position, and the left half (lanes 16-30) for standing. Early in races such as the mass start all athletes are bunched together from the get go with all lanes being devoted to a single shooting position. In other events such as the individual and sprint competitions where athletes start one after another, biathletes are free to select a shooting lane (often the lane practiced on) for the corresponding shooting position, standing or prone. Just prior to a race, biathletes file into an enclosed area, which is often televised, for a rifle inspection including trigger weight, resistance, dimensions and shape of the rifle (e.g., the distance between the centerline of the barrel and the lower edge of the forestock must not exceed 140 mm and/or the cheek piece must not exceed 40 mm), and the correctness of advertising stickers.[3,8] Once the rifle inspection is deemed a pass by an IBU official, a small colored sticker with the athlete's bib number is placed on the front of the forestock near the straight pull action as extra insurance that the rifle is within specs.

One by one they come into the shooting range skiing at a relaxed tempo, trying to lower heart and breathing rates to manageable levels. Gliding on both skis over snow recently groomed by an IBU official, competitors begin a well-choreographed sequence of maneuvers, beginning with either unclipping or loosening and removing neoprene wrists straps and flipping the snow cover off the front sight. A quick reach up to flip open or remove goggles followed by placing both poles in one hand, directing them either between their legs or to one side, biathletes quickly approach their shooting lane as designated by their bib number (and/or as directed by an IBU official who indicates by hand which lane to enter). To slow down, competitors employ a snow plow where the tips of each ski are forced together into an upside down V shape which edges into the snow slowing forward momentum. Coming in at an angle, the skis hit a 6 ½' x 5' mat located on a level shooting ramp, the area where biathletes stand or lie down, and a sequence of shot preparation commences that only years of experience could make look so graceful. With head and eyes looking forward towards the target, biathletes like Valj Semerenko (image 6.4) will start to bend down in anticipation of first kneeling on the mat. Poles are typically dropped to the mat between the legs, to the side, or even on top of the calves as both hands come down to meet the mat. Now kneeling, the right hand comes up, reaching behind to the rifle barrel harnessed to the back while the left hand and arm are slid through the rifle harness on the same side. Legs are splayed out of necessity at about 90 degrees from one another to each side considering the rigidity of the boots and lengthy skis. The rifle is pulled over the right shoulder as the left hand is brought across the body to 'catch' the rifle near its balance point on the forestock. At the same moment, the right hand is released and allowed to grab a magazine from the stock which is placed into the rifle feeder. On subsequent visits to the range, this sequence is slightly modified; a spent magazine is removed from the feeder, placed into the stock, and a new full magazine is selected from three others and pushed into the feeder.

Still kneeling, Semerenko now positions the rifle downrange butt end towards the right shoulder and reaches with the right hand to the rifle sling which is hooked to the left arm cuff just beneath the shoulder. With the left hand against the hand stop and right hand bracing on the ground, she crouches down into the prone position on the mat. Using considerable core strength, her torso is lifted slightly off the mat to allow the right hand to position the buttplate against the shoulder. Right elbow now on the mat, the right hand rapidly moves into the firing position, closes the breech with the thumb, and then grasps the pistol grip. The index finger simultaneously moves into position on the trigger while the right eye is brought into line with and in close proximity to the rear sight, perhaps two inches away yet preference is all the athlete's own. With the muzzle extended across the firing line, the rifle is raised from below to sight the target and from the side, the bent arms seem to create a 'W' while supporting the upper body and rifle. Now in the ready fire position, all the elements of rifle fit, position, and aiming culminate with a well-controlled squeeze of the trigger while heart rate hovers very close to maximum. And to think that these athletes consciously attempt to shoot between beats of the heart, when heart rate is high enough to elicit three beats per second, is a misnomer. Every biathlete has their own breathing and firing sequence and may resemble initially taking up the first stage of the trigger while breathing in. As aiming at the slightly elevated (80-100 cm or roughly 2.5-3.0 feet above the shooting ramp) center of the target is fine-tuned, athletes breathe out, then in, and finally out to ½ to ⅔ capacity, stopping to hold their breath. It may be difficult at this point to completely stabilize any extraneous movements and athletes might fire within 1-2 seconds after the target comes into view through the sites.[4] Waiting too long disintegrates the sight picture through unwanted movements or fatigue causing in many cases a 'snap' firing movement rather than the preferred light and uniform squeeze of the trigger.

Image 6.4. Russian biathlete Valj Semerenko (foreground) in the prone shooting position as Gabriela Koukalova (CZE), having shot faster, skis away from her shooting lane at the Nove Mesto IBU World Cup in 2015. Note rifle racks along the fence in the background holding spare rifles for competitors should a problem arise. (Photo by Marten_House/Shutterstock.com)

Feedback from the target is immediate as the bullet travels the 50 meters distance in a fraction of a second. Target backgrounds are painted white and constructed of heavy-duty metal, containing sensitive electronics to detect the strike of a bullet. Note in image 6.5 below that there are five targets evenly spaced by about 250 mm (almost 10 inches) and in line with one another, with each target containing a larger and smaller black circle within. The larger circle (target) is 115 mm (4.5 inches) across in diameter, about the size of a softball, and is used during the standing shoot, while the smaller golf ball sized 45 mm (1.8 inches) target at center is used for the more stable prone shooting. Should a bullet hit the larger or smaller circle during the standing or prone shooting, respectively, sensors located behind the metal housing of the biathlon target register the force, which must be 0.45 Ns (one newton second corresponds to one newton force or the force needed to accelerate 1 kg of mass at the rate of 1 meter per second, applied for one second; roughly the force that an egg makes if dropped from a height of 1 meter) or greater, and send an impulse to a servo-motor which flips up a white lollipop-like flap or slides a white metal flap from behind to cover the target. A bullet may on occasion hit the metal edge surrounding the target, fragmenting into what is called a "split shot", which may or may not activate the sensor with sufficient force to register a hit. To avoid any such ambiguity, a direct hit with a force not to exceed 1.0 Ns (placing limits on rifle power), according to IBU rules, is the goal of each biathlete.[3]

Image 6.5. Biathlon target showing white metal background that houses standing and prone (small darker circle within larger black circle) targets. Biathletes take one shot at each of the five targets moving from left to right, right to left, or in some other preferred combination. Each hit moves a hinged flap up from below to cover the target providing instant feedback for biathletes, coaches, and fans alike. Shooting lane 25 is clearly indicated in black and yellow to avoid cross lane shots. Note the bullet strikes around each target that have missed their mark. Several companies (see bibliography notes), including long standing HoRa Systemtechnik GmbH (GER) and Suomen Biathlon Oy (FIN), are approved by IBU to supply biathlon targets[3]. (Photo by 1599686sv/Shutterstock.com)

With each shot, information from the target is digitally transferred to timing, data, and TV interfaces, the latter displaying a graphic for TV viewers and fans at the stadium as to which targets were hit or missed by each athlete. Graphics designed for TV and also shown on the stadium big screen display an animated target, the athlete's name, and their home country. Each hit is noted with a white circle covering a target on the animation while a miss generates a red flash, leaves the target black, and produces a yellow dot next to the athlete's name indicating the total number of misses for that shooting. When the camera is isolated on one athlete in particular, the elapsed time passed until the first and between subsequent shots may be flashed above the target animation on the screen giving the audience an indication of how quickly (or not) shots were taken.

After each shot, a quick flick of the wrist pulls on the index finger, slides the straight action lever rearward, and ejects the spent cartridge from the chamber. The thumb then almost immediately closes the sliding breech on a new bullet. The only detectable movements by the biathlete come from breathing between shots, on a cold day even visualized as condensation, otherwise all body parts ideally remain motionless. After the last shot, a quick flip of the rear site cover with the right hand protects the sight from snow as the competitor presses up. Back to the knees now, the right hand is threaded through the harness strap, grabs the rifle barrel, and is hurtled in a controlled manner over the right shoulder. The left hand too is almost simultaneously passed through the harness strap on the opposite side while the right hand might, but not in all cases, close the front sight snow cover. A reach to the poles gathers all remaining equipment as the biathlete powerfully rises to their feet. Prior to securing pole straps, athletes will hop step off the mat, flip goggles back into place, plant the poles and ski away from their lane to generate forward momentum. Only then will the pole straps be clipped back in place or secured around the wrist to minimize time spent at the range. Out of the range, it's exit stage right and briskly up to speed on course if a clean shoot or exit stage left in most races (e.g., individual race is one minute time penalty for each missed shot rather than a penalty loop) for a counterclockwise ski of the penalty loop as punishment for any missed shots. At a position immediately after the penalty loop, athletes on course pass a time check which is tripped by their transponder to display on TV and the stadium big screen their time behind the leader. Athletes will sometimes be seen taking a peek at the big screen to confirm their lead or contemplate what kind of effort might be required to close a gap in the search for a win or podium spot.

On rare occasions, Murphy's Law is put into effect at the range as biathletes become panicked with a malfunctioning magazine or rifle. Should a magazine fail in the middle of shooting, a biathlete may load a new one or insert individual bullets carried on the rifle stock into the chamber to finish any remaining shots. In the event of a lost or completely malfunctioning magazine, competitors signal a nearby IBU range official by yelling "ammunition!" for a replacement.[3] Three staff members from each national federation are as well nearby in a cordoned off area directly behind IBU officials. In addition to extra magazines on hold which can be handed to an IBU official, coaches will be seen using high powered spotting scopes to determine the shot pattern of each biathlete. That information is digitally recorded for future use in training but also for real-time feedback which is relayed via two-way radio to staff. Out on course, a team staff member will run up to 50 meters (this is an IBU rule but who's really counting?) beside their athlete with the shot pattern or grouping, using five numbered circular magnets, displayed in the same pattern on a small magnetic board. Biathletes can then adjust their sights accordingly if a noticeable pattern (e.g., most shots low, or left, etc.) exists over the five shots.

TWO SKIS AND A RIFLE: AN INTRODUCTION TO BIATHLON

Image 6.6. Czech Republic national biathlon federation coach using spotting scope to note location of biathlete's shooting pattern. Pattern is digitally recorded and relayed via two-way radio to staff out on course. Note IBU officials and biathletes shooting in both prone and standing positions at the range (blurred) in the background. (Photo by Petr Toman/Shutterstock.com)

If a rifle jams or worse, is broken by a fall out on course, an athlete may ask for assistance at the range to make repairs but at this point, it's often faster to request a spare rifle. Similar to a magazine request, biathletes must raise their arm to acknowledge a range official and yell "rifle!" to indicate a spare is needed from the two allowed for each national federation. The IBU official will hurriedly proceed to the appropriate rifle rack of the national federation in question, grab a rifle, and run to the biathlete now positioned in his/her shooting lane. All of this of course takes extra time that may not be subtracted afterwards, and if that wasn't bad luck enough, most spare rifles are best fitted to top national federation athletes so rifle position will be off for most, leading to poor shooting. Contingencies also exist for malfunctioning targets, such as closing the lane, scoring hits if the target flap or plate fails, or resetting the targets on lane cross fires, but these problems are so rare as to hardly ever be observed.[3]

As the field separates with each lap, biathletes tend to come into the range more sporadically with some already in position or in the process of exiting. With the assistance of an IBU official, skiers will crisscross in front of or behind one another into their shooting lane. The standing position presents a less stable platform for shooting, yet it takes athletes about the same amount of time to complete all five shots as the prone shoot. Approaching the lane, a similar pattern for the standing shoot ensues with athletes gliding towards the lane, poles are removed and may be switched between the right and left hands as goggles and sights are flipped open. A flap on the glove covering the trigger finger is pulled back with the teeth to expose bare skin which enhances tactility between the index finger and trigger blade. Breathing rapidly now, athletes try to relax their cardiorespiratory system moments before snowplowing at a slight angle into the mat. A couple of quick steps on the mat sets the skis shoulder width apart in an open V position at slightly less than 45 degrees, left side of the body (for a right-handed shooter) facing somewhat perpendicular to the target. Poles are dropped between the legs onto the mat. A reach behind with the right

TWO SKIS AND A RIFLE: AN INTRODUCTION TO BIATHLON

hand secures the rifle barrel, while the left arm threads from behind and through the harness strap. With neutral body weight on both skis, the rifle is swung around the right shoulder as the arm slips out of the harness as the left hand shoots across the body to greet the rifle forestock.

A quick flick of the lever action ejects any remaining cartridge, the spent magazine is removed from the feeder, and a new one is inserted while the left hand supports the rifle. The rifle is rapidly secured against the right shoulder, while the left hand moves into position on the customized stock shape in front of the trigger well. The left thumb is often seen pressing up into the trigger well and along with the other fingers resembles holding a serving tray from beneath. Rifle now pointing towards the sky, the left elbow drops to the left hip to secure the arm in a relaxed manner to the body, creating a stable platform. Some will go so far as to lift their racing bib out of the way to expose allowable non-slip material designed to increase the friction between elbow and hip. With the rifle now in position and aiming towards the target, the head is canted forward and locked in position as sighting commences. The right arm is raised up to near parallel with the ground which serves to increase the 'pocket' for the buttplate to shoulder interface.[4] What ensues is a breathing sequence similar to the prone shooting where athletes partially exhale and engage the first stage of the trigger while drawing the rifle downwards into sight of the target. When the sight picture is ideal, the brain processes in a fraction of a second that it's go-time and with a squeeze of the trigger and flick of the straight pull action, five shots are fired in rapid succession as 1-2 breaths are taken between each shot. The rifle is dropped into the left hand, swung to the right, and both arms are fed through the harness to secure the rifle to the back. A reach to pick up the poles concludes the standing shoot as athletes hastily exit the range and ski to their destiny, a fate which is displayed on the big screen for all to see including time behind at the finish and number of missed shots (e.g., over the course of four shootings in a given race, the number of misses might be displayed as 2+1+3+0 for a total of six misses).

Image 6.7. Gabriela Koukalova and Darya Domracheva (left to right in foreground) during a standing shoot at Nove Mesto in 2015. Note microphones ahead of the firing line in each shooting lane to emphasize for fans in the stadium and on TV athletes laboring to breathe, reactions to missed shots, and the rifle report. (Photo by Marten-House/Shutterstock.com)

The clock never stops for a biathlete when underway which presents a rather unique dichotomy of shooting fast yet accurately. Many an Olympic shooting competition places a premium on accuracy, and while timed, the pressure to advance through several shots in rapid succession, particularly while undertaking high intensity endurance activity, is absent. Susan Dunklee has over the years analyzed this conundrum as she explains after her silver medal performance in the 2017 World Championship mass start race.

> Repetition and discipline and training will get you to be able to shoot fast in the race. And you have to get to the point where you trust that speed is better than shooting slow. That takes a long time, and one of the things that I have done this year is shooting on paper with speed, just to get used to that rhythm, and feel comfortable with that speedy rhythm. It has worked some days in races this year, and then other days it has totally fallen apart. But today it worked.[9]

Remarkably, the most accurate shooters on the biathlon World Cup, athletes like Vanessa Voigt (GER) and America's own Lowell Bailey are able to shoot successfully over 90% of the time on the year, approaching 500 total shots along the way.[10] All this is accomplished while hastily, yet deliberately firing off shots as they will know that time can be made up at the range that might be lost from skiing on course. Premier shooters like Simon Eder (AUT), while at times outside the top 20 in accuracy among the top competitors, spend very little time on the range, opening with their first of five shots in less than 12 seconds after hitting the mat. At the 2017 World Championships for example, Eder's first shot during a standing shoot came at 11.6 seconds, shot 2 came 1.8 seconds later, shot 3 - 4.9 sec, shot 4 – 4.6 sec, and the last at 3 sec for a total elapsed time under 26 seconds. And that was during the individual race where athletes tend to slow their shooting because of the disproportionately penal one minute time penalty for a miss (recall a penalty loop comparably costs 20-25 seconds lost time). At the Kontiolahti World Cup sprint competition in 2014, Eder in the standing position fired off his first round in less than 10 seconds upon entering his shooting lane, and exited in an astounding time of 17 seconds, taking just over 1 second per shot! Shoot quickly and it may pay off with a faster finishing time or enable a slower skier to catch a rival for a draft when exiting the range; however, the risk of a miss is heightened and athletes will often weigh the pros and cons of such mid-race.

The fastest women shooters on the World Cup circuit, athletes like Julia Simon (FRA) or Dorothea Wierer (ITA) spend about 27 seconds on the shooting mat in the prone position, and slightly less when standing (23 or 25 seconds, respectively). These times for Simon and Wierer are 4-5 seconds faster than the field average and the slight difference of roughly three seconds between prone and standing shooting is invariably due to time lost maneuvering the body to the ground and regaining a stance. When analyzing the top 90 shooters in the field who have accumulated at least six races over the season, men shoot slightly faster than women, about two seconds for both the prone and standing positions on average. However, many a woman spends less time on the range than her male counterpart which presents an interesting parity in the sport of biathlon. The average range time for top biathletes over the course of a year varies quite considerably and most take about 52 seconds (women) and 48 seconds (men) to ski into the range, complete each shooting, and then exit. The fastest competitors, like Eder and Simon, may exit the range a full six seconds faster than average, time that might never be made up by a rival competitor on a clean shooting day.[11]

Chapter Seven
Competing Clean Means Year-Round Training

Nordic skiers are often considered to be the fittest endurance athletes on the planet. Many other sports like running, cycling, and triathlon utilize muscles in a particular region of the body, or in the case of triathlon, one region at a time. Nordic skiing on the other hand *simultaneously* over long distances combines large muscle groups of the upper (poling) and lower (skiing) extremities as a requirement for the sport. For that reason, the cardiorespiratory, muscular, and metabolic systems of an elite Nordic skier adapt more so than in athletes from other endurance-oriented endeavors. Biathletes are no different and many an elite competitor, like Ole Einar Bjoerndalen, have exhibited similar aerobic endurance capacities as their Nordic skiing peers. Recently and in the interest of transparency following the revelations uncovered within the McLaren Report, national federations like Norway have released physiological data of their top Olympic athletes to the delight of governing bodies and physiologists the world over. The release of this information may usher in a new era of scientific candor and foster comparative physiological testing of biathletes who hope to one day reach the pinnacle of the sport.

Skiing performance or more specifically speed is determined by two factors; 1) the energy turnover, or the relationship of energy used by an athlete in the form of carbohydrates and/or fat and, 2) work economy, or work efficiency such that improvements in technique will *reduce* the energy required for skiing. Improve either one of these factors, and the athlete will see dividends of improved performance. Energy turnover and work economy are largely determined in a laboratory setting using an analyzer that measures the amount of oxygen being utilized by an athlete. A greater ability to breathe in and physiologically utilize oxygen translates to improved energy turnover because it reduces unwanted energy from anaerobic ('without' oxygen) systems which ultimately are depleted sooner and may cause unwanted fatigue. Elite Nordic skiers and biathletes demonstrate exceptional abilities for oxygen utilization which is characterized by maximal aerobic capacity or VO_{2max} (V = volume, O_2 = oxygen, max = maximal value achieved).[1,2]

Not since the mid-1960's has there been more data released on the maximal aerobic capacities of winter Olympic athletes than in a 2015 study published in the International Journal of Sports Physiology and Performance. What had long been held in confidence by athletes and physiologists, who often were employed by national federations to test athletes in house, Espen Tonnesen and colleagues definitively released data from Olympic medalists in several winter sports from the time period 1990 to 2013. A few take aways from this study were that both men and women cross-country skiers who were medalists during the study time period had the highest VO_{2max} values of 84.3 and 72.5 $mL \cdot kg^{-1} \cdot min^{-1}$, respectively. This means that these athletes were able to consume and utilize 6½ (men) or 4¼ (women) liters (think of a 1 liter soda/seltzer bottle) of oxygen per minute; incredible when average values one-half these are the norm for non-athletes. Medalist biathletes were not far behind their cross-country counterparts with values of 81.1 and 65.9 $mL \cdot kg^{-1} \cdot min^{-1}$ for men and women, respectively, illustrating the prodigious aerobic demands of the sport. Interestingly, non-medaling biathletes differed by just slightly more than 3 $mL \cdot kg^{-1} \cdot min^{-1}$ than their podium rivals.[3] What this suggests is that while it is imperative to maximize aerobic capacity through a combination of genetics (non-modifiable) and training (modifiable), other factors like shooting or skiing technique, variables that are

TWO SKIS AND A RIFLE: AN INTRODUCTION TO BIATHLON

independent of VO_{2max} alone, play increasing roles as elite athletes search for biathlon success.

The effectiveness of skiing technique is aptly determined through analysis of the O_2 cost of the activity. Essentially, there appears to be a strong relationship between the O_2 cost of cross-country skiing and performance.[1] O_2 cost refers to the metabolic demands required to sustain physical activity for prolonged periods of time and, along with VO_{2max}, is measured using a machine that analyzes breathed gases during exercise. Treadmills with considerably more surface area than what one might find at the local gym, are used to test Nordic skiers and biathletes while using roller-skis which are modified skis with roller blade-like wheels on either end. Athletes are harnessed on the upper body and ski, very much as they normally do, using poles and skating technique as the treadmill increases in speed and gradient (see image 7.1). O_2 cost at any given treadmill speed and VO_{2max}, once fatigue is reached and the athlete slips backwards on the treadmill to be caught by the harness, are determined using the apparatus. Other and more common modes of fitness testing utilize bicycle ergometers or common walking/running treadmills and tend to incorporate measurements such as lactate, a by-product of anaerobic metabolism, which determines how well the aerobic system is functioning. That may seem counterintuitive but the more lactate produced by the body at any given exercise intensity below maximal level, the lesser reliance on the preferred aerobic system. Or in other words, biathletes who can delay the onset of blood lactate formed by metabolic processes in muscle, which is largely dictated by O_2 cost and VO_{2max}, have an advantage over others and can ski at higher velocities before fatigue sets in.

Hypothetically, let's say former Olympian biathletes and teammates Clare Egan and Susan Dunklee have a similar VO_{2max} and are skiing side by side during a race. Egan has a current O_2 cost, the amount of oxygen being consumed in real time at some fraction of her maximal value, of 50 mL·kg^{-1}·min^{-1} whereas Dunklee was consuming oxygen at a rate of 47 mL·kg^{-1}·min^{-1}. Which of the two biathletes O$_2$ cost was lower, owing in theory to better technique? Dunklee, with her lower O$_2$ cost, wastes less energy when propelling her body forward which could reduce lactate production, delay the onset of fatigue, and/or provide extra energy later for a sprint finish. When biathletes are seen sprinting to the line or up a hill or are simply trying to 'hang on' to a faster skier, a primary source of energy comes from somewhat limited stores of glucose which forms lactate via anaerobic metabolism rather than a mixture of fat/glucose (called a glycogen sparing effect) observed during aerobic metabolism. That is why biathletes will switch to V1 technique on steeper uphill sections instead of remaining in V2 which increases O$_2$ cost on hilly terrain and may call upon anaerobic processes moreso.[1] Improvements in lactate profile (e.g., when blood lactate begins to increase appreciably at a certain exercise intensity), O$_2$ cost, and/or VO$_{2max}$ come from years of training and racing at the highest level, and to think that biathletes have an 'off season' is somewhat misleading. Training camps are a regular part of a biathlete's yearly calendar, even in between races during the competitive season, and athletes will often travel to distant locations to meet their teammates for extended periods of conditioning work.

Image 7.1. Athlete undergoing laboratory fitness test on a roller-ski treadmill. Numerous tests can be performed including gradually increasing exercise intensity to a maximal effort while monitoring O_2 cost and/or the highest recorded oxygen consumption value; noted as VO_{2max} or sometimes VO_{2peak}. Note the safety harness and cord attached to the athlete's waist and torso in case of a fall or when dropping off the pace due to fatigue. (Photo courtesy of Dan Heil, Ph.D., FACSM, Montana State University – Bozeman, MT, USA)

...

There is little time for the professional biathlete to become too accustomed to life away from the sport after the competitive season has closed. Within a few weeks, athletes are early in their periodization training plan, a training regimen that modifies exercise frequency, intensity, time, or type utilizing blocks or cycles divided into weeks and months over the course of a year. Spending time at training camps and working towards goals prescribed by coaches is what Clare Egan expected to experience in the early stages of training at the conclusion of one Word Cup season and the start of another.

> The first few weeks are indeed physically arduous, but the bigger challenge for me is the psychological stress that comes with renouncing a balanced life. During the coming 11 months, I will spend about 230 days on the road, train 6 days/week, and commit 24 hours/day to optimal health and recovery.[4]

For several seasons now, the Americans have traveled to Bend, Oregon in early May to ski on the several feet of accumulated snow at the Mt. Bachelor Nordic Center. Here they will ski for hours each morning and supplement their 'base' conditioning with running or cycling cross-training in the afternoon. At this point in the season, physical training is focused on general aerobic conditioning with sufficient rest, recovery, and nutrition to prevent early burnout. As an athlete ramps up their training volume, she/he will expend more calories to sustain physical activity, and thus proper nutrition will need to compensate for this increased caloric demand. Focusing on carbohydrate rich foods like grains, pasta, and fruit help to replenish lost glycogen (our storage form of glucose or carbohydrate) stores in the muscle, which is the preferred fuel for higher intensity aerobic exercise.

Summertime presents a unique challenge for Nordic skiing athletes and with snow in scarce quantity, alternate forms of dry land training that simulate skating technique are sought out. Enter roller-skiing. Using wheels resembling those found on roller blades/skates, although slightly wider and attached to narrow platforms similar to cross-country skis, biathletes can train on pavement using skating techniques which nearly mimic the real thing. Poles have modified metal tips that bite into pavement while boots, clipped into familiar bindings, have enhanced breathability collectively equipping athletes for the double poling V skate. In fact, the IBU has placed such great emphasis on roller-skiing that annually a summer world championships is held often at one of the same venues that plays host to a winter World Cup biathlon race. Several top winter biathletes, like Mara Laukkanen and Kaisa Makarainen, trained with such regularity on roller-skis that in years past they've podiumed or even won outright the Summer Biathlon World Championships. For most winter biathletes warm weather roller-skiing is *the* primary mode of conditioning the major bodily systems in anticipation of a return to snow skis.

Image 7.2. Svetlana Sleptsova (RUS) seen here in the pursuit race dominated the 2017 Summer Biathlon World Championships in Chaykovskiy, Russia. (Photo by Julia_Sadykova/Shutterstock.com)

As the 'off-season' reaches the summer months, athletes from various national federations will often serendipitously encounter one another at European training camps. Tronstad, Norway hosts a roller-skiing festival each July and several of the world's top biathletes from Canada, Finland, USA, Russia, and Norway have rendezvoused for bouts of roller-skiing and shooting practice leading into competition at the festival. At other times, training happens on home soil, and for Americans, that means relocating to Lake Placid, NY or Craftsbury, VT for roller-skiing, running, cycling, and weight training.[5] But for some, traveling to simply train, particularly overseas, is not always enjoyable earning the moniker "draining camps". Egan described the changes in physical and psychological status over a 17 day training camp beginning with "sanatiz[ing] all surfaces and self" and "procurement of own food" in the early days, to "wonder[ing] how it is possible to feel so bad, when felt so good yesterday" at about half way, and towards the end of camp, "tak[ing] a nap on the road during practice."[6] The physical training load and mental stress of co-habitating with other athletes and coaches with limited social outlets (often camps are in remote locations) can wreak havoc on an athlete's psyche.

Training in an Olympic year has even greater importance, particularly for smaller teams who work in relative obscurity alongside powerhouses like Germany, France, and Norway. Typically, as the World Cup season draws closer and closer, training ramps up as Lithuanian coach Meelis Aasmae explained.

> We do not train too much at home. This year our camps included Otepää and Pokljuka and now here in Obertilliach. After this, we will go to Raubichi for a camp and the Belarusian Championships, then to Ramsau in mid-October to ski on the glacier. Just before the season starts, our on-snow camp will be in Sjusjøen.[7]

TWO SKIS AND A RIFLE: AN INTRODUCTION TO BIATHLON

Two- and one-half hour training sessions are the norm for these athletes, focusing on longer intervals, bursts of high intensity, and shooting drills/practice. Lactate testing is very common to ensure athletes maintain prescribed exercise intensities and avoid overtraining, which can see an athlete regress by several weeks if training volume is not properly monitored. Yet peaking for a particular event such as the World Championships or Olympics is very difficult as Italian coach Patrick Oberegger discussed in his non-native English tongue.

> Over the years, we noticed that it is extremely hard to time everything so that athletes reach the highest of their form in a specific week. Our ideas is that, if the team functions well from the beginning of the season, and that means not just getting good results. It also involves how the relationship with coaches, physiotherapists, and everything goes. Then, it is so much easier for them to find their best form at the right moment.[8]

Autumn brings cooler temperatures and the approach of a new World Cup season, and teams are now faced with preparing athletes who have not been on snow for several months. The solution; glacier skiing and Nordic skiing snow tunnels. In a typical year, biathletes from the United States plan a snow training camp after which the women's and men's World Cup team or "A Team" is named. Meanwhile in Europe, many teams make the Val Senales Glacier in South Tyrol their home for several weeks, which offers the advantage of being situated at 3,000 meters (almost 10,000 feet!) above sea level.[9] Coaches and athletes will know that oxygen molecules are more widely dispersed at altitude as atmospheric pressure drops. Stay long enough and the body is stimulated to upregulate erythropoiesis or the generation of new red blood cells in bone marrow. And while not the ideal 'live high, train low' scenario that is common practice for the endurance athlete, practicality dictates that biathletes live *and* train at high altitude thus potentially hindering training stimulus (it's simply harder to exercise at altitude), yet it still offers the advantage of increased red blood cell production. The end result for athletes is several post weeks of improved oxygen carrying capacity from blood to muscle which enhances VO_{2max} and thus endurance performance.

Indoor ski tunnels with near perfect temperature control and ease of waxing, groomed skate and classic tracks, and some even containing a biathlon range, offer year-round skiing and training for biathletes. It goes without saying that when snow is available only at high altitude and/or latitude, snow tunnels deliver a viable alternative for cross-country skiers and biathletes to practice on the real thing. About two hours outside of Oslo is Torsby, Sweden, home to the Fortum Ski Tunnel. The U.S. Biathlon Team has come to Torsby in the fall as preparation for the World Cup, skiing its 1.3 km loop which offers elevation changes to hone various skating techniques. A weight room for developing core strength, the muscles in and around the torso which are used for stability, poling, posture, and just about everything else biathlon, is a common training destination between ski training. Outside the tunnel is a roller-skiing track and miles of trails and hills to suffer through hill bounding, a method of training where athletes jump up hills using poles as propulsion to develop upper body strength. Oberhof, Germany offers a similar indoor skiing center with the advantage of indoor biathlon ranges for both roller-skiing and snow skiing. At a cost of 14 million Euro ($15.75 million), the tunnel floor is cooled by pipes inserted into concrete while the room air is held constant at -3 to -4 degrees Celsius (25-27 degrees Fahrenheit). Snow machines under the ceiling vaporize water and compressed air and by dropping it from a height of eight meters (26 feet), snow crystals are formed.[10] Finland is the leader in indoor Nordic skiing, with six tunnels spread across the country. After a day on the ski loop, Nordic skiers and biathletes may head for a sauna, which some believe aids in recovery by removing toxins from the body, interspersed with cold water immersion which releases 'feel-good' endorphins.[11]

...

Being on the road is a way of life for the World Cup biathlete, and finding time or more importantly a biathlon range for daily practice is challenging. Dry firing, or practicing with the rifle without using live ammunition, is part of every biathlete's repertoire because it can be done almost anywhere. After removing the straight pull bolt action on the rifle, the firing pin, a small rod that makes contact with the primer on the cartridge, is exposed and a small donut or a "tone down disc" can be inserted to allow dry firing without damaging the firing chamber. Concentration is necessary to maximize the benefits of dry fire training and often a biathlete's hotel or dorm room will feature pieces of paper with small hand drawn black circles taped to a wall, simulating the five biathlon targets on a shooting range. Exercises might begin with visualization, an imaging technique that attempts to incorporate all senses into a 'feeling', of prone and standing shooting and/or other exercises to develop balance and stability. After the visualization task and still sitting quietly, getting a feel now for the first and second stages of the trigger eases the mind and body into more strenuous exercises. Numerous exercises have been developed like slow shooting, fast shooting, adding weight to the barrel or elbow, shooting with eyes closed, target approach drills, and a "5-bull drill" which may gradually progress to a point of dry firing under exercise conditions. Ultimately, a repeatable pattern of bodily steadiness and trigger pressure during competition are pursued to smoothly engage the sear of trigger engagement (see Image 7.3 below). Breathing becomes more and more important as physical activities like running or push-ups are integrated into dry firing routines.[12] And while the psychological pressure of a race is difficult to replicate, shooting while breathing heavily and with a high heart rate similar to race conditions (the heart rate of a biathlete may approach 190 beats per minute when entering a shooting lane during a race which may be as much as 140 beats above their resting heart rate!), is an essential component to training.

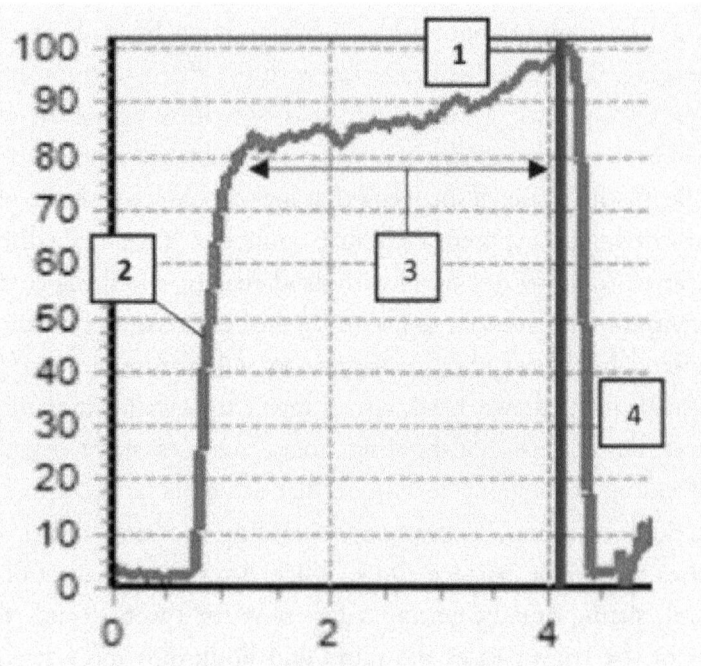

Image 7.3. Image of an ideal trigger force curve. The vertical axis represents the percentage of force being applied to the trigger prior to trigger break (or 100% force). The horizontal axis represents time in seconds. Along the curve are phases leading up to the shot. Phase 2 represents a rapid increase of force on the trigger up to about 80%. Phase 3 is a plateau in force where the biathlete holds tension against the trigger ideally between 80-90% for a brief period of time. Phase 1 should require little effort to produce the extra 10-20% effort to break

the sear of engagement and avoids 'jerking' of the trigger. After the shot, the finger is smoothly removed from the trigger in phase 4 and the process is repeated. (Image with permission by Sattlecker, G., Edfelder, J., and Gressenbauer, C. and the International Biathlon Union. From the Exercise Catalogue for Biathlon Shooting)[35]

Shooting coaches are the norm for national federations, and USA Biathlon certainly agrees having in past acquiring the services of experts like Matt Emmons who set to help national team members prepare during the lead up to the PyeongChang Winter Olympics. A four time Olympian and three time medalist himself, Emmons brought a wealth of technical experience to the table and a love for coaching, a perfect combination for the U.S. Biathlon Team. Arguably, Emmons played a role in the recent successes of Bailey and Dunklee at the 2017 World Championships who along with Tim Burke have sought his advice on the sometimes minute details of shooting. Dunklee credited Emmons with subtly changing her position on the range.

> He helped a lot in my standing position getting more stable. I always had a position where I leaned forward on my toes a little, and it put me a little off-balance. He had a couple small suggestions, very simple things, but things that coaches had never thought to point out before, and it really changed things for me.[13]

But it's controlling the mental aspect of shooting mid-race when confronted with controlling the pressure of trying to outclass 29 other biathletes at either side, rifle reports in each ear, heart rate soaring, breathing nearly out of control, cold temperature, wind, and possibly snowy conditions, that Emmons, now the shooting coach for the Czech national team, is what coaches hope to instill in athletes to bring them to the highest level of the sport. And while not all shooting coaches are biathletes themselves, Emmons believed the mental fortitude that brought him success in 50 meter shooting at the Olympics would convey to U.S. biathletes.

> I have a long competition history behind me with a lot of success, but I've also had to overcome and deal with some pretty tough stuff throughout my career. From my experience, being mentally tough and simply doing the right things psychologically to be successful doesn't depend much on the sport. Those skills carry over regardless of the sport, and even in life or business.[13]

While the torch has passed from Emmons to a new coaching staff, including Lowell Bailey and Tim Burke among others within U.S. Biathlon, to toughen the mind and improve confidence in high pressure situations, coaches will often prescribe a training drill that attempts to simulate shooting at some high stakes competition in what is known as a 'podium test'. As Dunklee describes, "the goal was to hit a certain percentage of the targets in under a certain amount of time, which they had calculated would be a medal-winning performance for us."[14] Later that season at the 2014 Sochi Winter Olympic Games, she would put that training to the test in the pursuit race.

> I entered the range immediately behind the 3rd and 4th place athletes. We had a head-to-head shooting battle, the most exciting and high pressure type, and unfortunately I finished with some trips around the penalty loop and lost several places. It was a disappointing ending, but after the race one of my coaches was quick to point out that I had gotten to do a "real, live podium test at the Olympics." Pretty cool.[14]

Pretty cool indeed. It's interesting to note that while Dunklee entered the range very close behind her nearest competitor, the deciding turn of events was accuracy. Contemporary thought suggests that little time can be gained overall if shooting time is reduced, but improving accuracy and limiting trips around the penalty loop can have drastic implications on final race position.[15] That is precisely the reason why biathletes tend to alter minor details in their shooting position from year to year like avoiding canting to one side, bending the knees too much which may cause early onset of fatigue, or over-holding the rifle while maximizing foot placement, breathing patterns, and balance.[12]

Image 7.4. Susan Dunklee (USA) competing in the 7.5 km sprint race at the Sochi 2014 Winter Olympic Games. Dunklee would subsequently win a silver medal at the 2020 World Championships in the sprint race. (Photo by Iurii Osadchi/Shutterstock.com)

One way biathletes eliminate any X-factor affecting shooting accuracy is to keep their rifles in tip top shape. Rifle cleaning is a common ritual performed by all the top biathletes and is not only good practice, but may, by getting to know every nut and bolt, psychologically strengthen the bond between athlete and tool of the trade. Rifles are constantly exposed to the elements from wind born dust and grit to rain, snow, and/or general humidity all of which can break down oil or deteriorate metal on the many moving parts of a biathlon rifle. Biathletes will travel with a cleaning kit containing several accessories including a flexible snake tool onto which a brush is attached, cotton patches, and a degreasing and cleaning solution. After removing the Fortner bolt, the snake and brush assembly is fed through the bore towards the top or fore sight end of the rifle, making a few passes to ensure all heavier grit is removed. Using the same snake tool, a cotton patch is then attached with cleaning solution applied and fed in the same way through the barrel to catch any fine particulate matter. A lubricant is applied to a microfiber cleaning cloth and rubbed onto all exposed surfaces of the rifle to prevent pitting or rust formation. The final step is to clean the bolt itself using an instrument resembling a shortened dental pick which can be lightly scraped into any small crevices that would otherwise be difficult to access with a cleaning rag. Once the bolt action has been wiped down with light oil, the pick is used to clean the barrel near the bore of any remaining grime.[16] Some will go so far as to completely remove the barrel and trigger assembly from the rifle to more thoroughly clean hidden areas enshrouded by the stock. Magazines are also inspected and cleaned as necessary to prevent jams while shooting, which if such an unlikely event occurred would require the time delaying assistance of an IBU official on the range.

Image 7.5. Snake tool and cotton wick used to clean the barrel of a biathlon rifle. Special oil may be applied to the wick before it is threaded into and pulled through the barrel. (Photo courtesy of J.G. Anschütz GmbH & Co. KG)

...

Like most Olympic sports, the IBU has "emphasized clean sport, the fight against doping and protection of clean athletes as its top priorities." In 2003, the IBU first adhered to the World Anti-Doping Association (WADA) code and in a joint effort between WADA, the Biathlon Integrity Unit (BIU) established by the IBU in 2021, and national federation anti-doping associations, like the United States Anti-Doping Association (USADA), coordinate "the universal fight against doping in sport."[17] And while great efforts are made to educate athletes and officials on the spirit of sport, in part characterized by ethics, health, teamwork, character, and respect for self and others, biathlon has not been entirely immune to controversy surrounding fair play. Society often villainizes a single athlete as a rogue doper acting autonomously in the quest for athletic gains; however, in reality it is more often a coordination of efforts between athlete, coach, doctor, and/or at the highest level, government authority.

The era of the East German sports program, long associated with systematic performance enhancing drug experimentation, began in the late 1960's, not long after the availability of testosterone, steroids, and growth hormones became more widely available to the general public after advances in human biology and medicine.[18] Until that time, stimulants such as amphetamines or cocaine, which give a euphoric high to push aside the physical and mental sensations of pain associated with strenuous exercise, were the drug of choice for athletes. Alongside the East German sporting regime, Soviet scientists were reportedly undertaking their own experiments on the effectiveness of hormone use to improve sporting performance. Perfectly healthy athletes at the 1956 World Games in Moscow were seen using catheters in order to urinate, a side effect of an enlarged prostate due to testosterone use. Having learned of this effective performance aid, pharmaceutical companies in collaboration with scientists developed Dianabol in the United States which will be remembered as the first 'big-time' anabolic steroid used by American athletes.[19] By the 1960's anabolic steroids like Dianabol were widely incorporated into sport for their ability to increase protein metabolism in muscle and for reducing cortisol levels which catabolize (break down as opposed to build up in anabolism; thus the term 'anabolic' steroids) muscle in times of stress, collectively increasing muscle mass in an athlete.

At the 1990 Minsk Biathlon World Championships, Frank writes that a Soviet regional paper reported on the problem of anabolic stimulant use as an effective means to become stronger during training.[18] That training effect would translate into improved performance in biathlon competition where less fatigue mid-race would increase ski speed and perhaps improve stability on the shooting range. The nature of biathlon presents a conundrum for any would be doper in that unethical drugs used to improve shooting accuracy would likely be a detriment to skiing performance. Thus, developments in performance enhancing aids in Nordic skiers would gain the attention of biathletes since the most significant benefits come from reduced skiing time on course rather than at the shooting range.

Blood doping, or the removal and subsequent reinfusing of blood back into the body, gained notoriety during the 1984 Olympic Games when several physicians blood doped the United States cycling team.[19] Earlier reports of blood doping at the 1980 Moscow Summer Games and from Finnish experiments on Nordic skiers at the 1984 Winter Olympic Games illustrated the effectiveness of strategically removing ones blood for improved endurance performance.[18] After a short period of time, the body compensates for the lost blood by boosting its own production in attempt to restore normal levels. Subsequent reinfusing of the athlete's own blood (autologous) or from a donor individual (homologous) would boost the number of red blood cells and thus improve oxygen carrying capacity. In effect, a Nordic skier could cut over two minutes time in a 10 km race after blood doping which could mean the difference between a podium placing or being an also-ran.[20]

Even though the process of blood doping would be banned after the 1984 Olympics, cases would periodically crop up at major international events. In 1992 Russian biathlete Sergei Tarasov was heralded as a favorite for the 20 km race at the Albertville Olympics. Just prior to the competition, he was hospitalized with what team officials claimed was food poisoning. However, the fact that he was treated with a kidney dialysis machine and corticosteroids led some to believe that this was a case of misguided blood doping. Tarasov would recover and go on to win the race, denying that he had ever competed after using blood doping.[21] In 2006 the IOC handed down its heaviest punishment of banishment for life to six Austrian Nordic athletes, including two biathletes, who were caught with blood bags, butterfly valves for intravenous infusion, saline, and a hemoglobin meter, which measures the ratio of red blood cells to fluid in the blood, at their apartment at the Turin Olympics.[22] Athletes in a never ending quest continued to search for advances in performance enhancing aids and would reap the benefits of scientific research after the advent of perhaps the single most influential drug in the history of endurance sport, erythropoietin or simply EPO.

EPO is a naturally occurring hormone that is released by the kidneys to stimulate red blood cell production in bone marrow. In the 1980's, researchers began exploring the possibility of producing exogenous (external source) EPO using recombinant DNA technology in cell cultures; essentially replicating EPO produced endogenously (internal source). The earliest form of recombinant human erythropoietin (rhEPO) would be used to correct anemia in cancer patients and would eventually find its way onto the doping black market. Quick to maneuver around the now banned blood doping, physiologists like Dr. Francesco Conconi began developing rhEPO use in athletes as a way to increase endurance performance.[19] Rumors of rhEPO surfaced at the 1984 Winter Olympics[18], but it would take until the late 1980's for its use to reach epidemic proportions as young Dutch cyclists began dying in their sleep because of suggested rhEPO polycythemia (high red blood cell count which increases the viscosity of blood) related complications. In fact, athletes using rhEPO would be instructed to wake several times at night and perform light exercise to increase their heart rate as a way to lessen the risk of blood clots. The IOC would ban rhEPO in 1990 but it and other more refined forms of EPO, like continuous EPO receptor activator, would plague modern sport for years to come. In fact in 2015, three Russian biathletes were handed suspensions by the IBU anti-doping panel for illicit use of rhEPO during the late 2013 biathlon season.[23] Even more recently, former IBU president Anders Besseberg has been accused of corruption by accepting bribes in the protection of Russia from doping cases during his leadership (through 2018) and is set to stand trial in early 2024. But none of these examples would compare to the revelation of state organized, systematic, and wide-spread doping outlined in the WADA sponsored McLaren Report that came out of the 2014 Sochi Winter Olympic Games.

On May 12, 2016, The New York Times ran an article claiming that Russian athletes were part of a state-sponsored doping program after whistleblower Dr. Grigory Rodchenkov, laboratory director for thousands of Olympians, described the operation and his detailed role in the process.[24] In what reads like a blockbuster movie script, the story begins several years prior to Sochi following the abysmal performance of Russian athletes at the 2010 Vancouver Winter Olympics. In Moscow, a WADA accredited anti-doping laboratory had been corrupted by the state to falsify any positive tests of Russian athletes as negative in the WADA anti-doping management system (ADAMS) in what was described as the "disappearing positive methodology". Subsequent to the disappearing positive allegations, thousands of samples were alleged to have been destroyed by the lab in Moscow.[25]

With the Sochi Olympics on the horizon, a novel method had been developed by the Russian Federal Security Service (FSB), successor of the KGB, to remove the supposedly tamper resistant caps from bottles used to collect urine and replace a suspected positive sample with a clean one. A clean urine bank was accumulated in parallel from athletes, who were instructed to provide samples after drug wash-out periods had passed, as a stockpile to guard against adverse analytical findings as they might present in Sochi. Once the clean urine bank was deemed sufficient, the FSB agent, operating in the middle of the night under the cover of a sewage and plumbing employee, would covertly transport the clean samples from Moscow to a storage freezer adjacent to the Sochi anti-doping laboratory.[25]

Years prior to the Sochi Olympics, Rodchenkov had developed a steroid cocktail mixed in alcohol that athletes could swish in their mouths to reap the benefits of the drugs with a more rapid wash out period (time to be undetectable) compared to injection. According to Rodchenkov, many athletes at Sochi were using his cocktail to compete dirty. He would then describe how A and B samples, all athletes undergoing doping control provide a sample which is placed into an A bottle with a stopper and B bottle with the 'tamper-proof' cap, were passed through a "mouse hole" from inside the secure Sochi laboratory to an unsecure FSB accessible operations room behind the wall. The FSB agent would take the B sample and leave the operations room, while clean urine from the storage room was brought to the operations room to thaw. The B sample was returned to the operations room with the cap removed, the sample was discarded, and then replaced with the now thawed clean urine. Upon also replacing the A sample with clean urine and adjusting for specific gravity (essentially the ratio of solid to liquid) to match the sample at initial collection, both the A and B samples would be passed by the FSB agent through the mouse hole back into the 'secure' anti-doping room to be received by a credentialed Russian lab employee who was in on the scheme. The standard laboratory procedure for analyzing samples was then performed by a random international technician unaware of any tampering, and the result was no adverse findings for any Russian athlete competing at Sochi.[25]

The ramifications that came out of the McLaren report were immense, and a list of 31 biathletes implicated in the report was provided to IBU. In January 2017, following a December 2016 meeting in which two biathletes were suspended, the IBU held a rare extraordinary meeting to discuss the results of the investigation and the fates of the remaining 29 athletes. Together with the Russian Biathlon Union (RBU), the IBU narrowed down the investigation to seven athletes, clearing 22 others who were implicated.[26] In mid-September 2017, WADA, citing that international federations including the IBU found insufficient evidence of rules violations, controversially dismissed the cases of 95 out of 96 Russian athletes, in the process perhaps clearing all remaining biathletes under investigation following the IBU and RBU collaborative investigation. Just one day after the news broke on September 12th, seventeen national doping agencies, including USADA, demanded that Russia be banned from the 2018 PyeongChang Winter Olympics.[27] In a statement released by USADA, the seventeen leaders under the name National Anti-Doping Organization (NADO) voiced their concern to the IOC over the handling of the investigation.

> The IOC needs to stop kicking the can down the road and immediately issue meaningful consequences. The failure to expeditiously investigate individual Russian athlete doping poses a clear and present danger for clean athletes worldwide and at the 2018 Winter Games. We have serious doubts that the 2018 Games will be clean due to the incomplete investigation of massive evidence of individual doping by Russians athletes at the 2014 Sochi Olympic Games and

given the inadequate testing evidence of Russian athletes over the past four years.[28]

NADO would only accept Russian athletes in PyeongChang who were not implicated in the state-sponsored doping scheme and were required to compete under a unified Olympic flag (which was extended through the 2022 Beijing Winter Olympics). In part and because of this unified voice of concern, the RBU and Russian Olympic Committee (ROC) both were and remain suspended by the IBU and the International Olympic Committee, respectively; a condition that must be cleared for its athletes to be able to compete in elite biathlon events like the World Cup and Olympic Games. The RBU has a long road ahead of itself and must meet a host of criteria such as paying for out of competition testing for biathletes, reimbursement of the IBU for legal fees associated with the McLaren investigation, and perhaps most significantly, release of data from the Moscow lab, before being reinstated.[36]

> The IOC and WADA must insist that Russia turn over this [Moscow lab data] key additional evidence. A full account and justice for clean athletes cannot be achieved without this information. The failure to properly investigate and prosecute free of sport-political influence those who violated anti-doping rules, breaks the trust with millions of clean athletes around the world. This dereliction of duty sends a cynical message that those of favored, insider nations within the Olympic Movement will never be punished or held accountable, violating the fundamental covenant of fairness on which sport is based.[28]

...

To be an elite athlete means being subject to random drug tests anywhere and anytime as Dunklee points out. "We have to submit our detailed whereabouts to anti-doping authorities. Occasionally their agents come knocking and collect urine and blood samples. It is an inconvenience that I gladly endure to keep our sport honest and clean."[29] The detailed whereabouts Dunklee refers to is run by WADA through the computer database program ADAMS. Athletes can log in and provide information about their whereabouts at all times, whether home training, abroad with the team at a training camp, where staying at any of the World Cup events, or the beach at which they'll be vacationing. There are several reasons why an athlete might be in violation of anti-doping rules including the use, attempted use, or presence of a prohibited substance or marker in a urine/blood sample, evading or failing to submit a sample, three missed tests or filing failures in a twelve month period, tampering with doping control, possession of prohibited substances, and association infractions like trafficking, complicity, or administering substances to another athlete.[30] The burden of proof in establishing a violation rests with the IBU and affiliated organizations like WADA, the newly created Biathlon Integrity Unit (BIU) and the international federation's home anti-doping agency like USADA, and unless there is sufficient evidence, the case against an athlete might likely be dropped.

In some situations, an athlete might be prescribed a drug for medicinal purposes that is on the WADA list of prohibited substances. In this case the athlete would submit what is called a therapeutic use exemption or TUE to the national federation and IBU. However, there are some who believe that nations or individual athletes might hide unethical performance enhancing drug (PED) use under the umbrella of a TUE. Doping scandals and questions of fair play continue to surface, including recently allegations that the Kazakhstan biathlon team was caught discarding drug paraphernalia at a gas station.[31]

Almost immediately the TUE white flag was raised; however, then IBU president Anders Besseberg (now Olle Dahlin from Sweden) was quick to point out that among the 1,000 or more biathletes competing at the international level, only four have TUE's.[32] New cases of doping continue to surface and was the reason behind the formation of the BIU, which holds all players accountable for their actions. In fact, athletes are now required to provide a certificate indicating that they have undergone a doping educational program.[34]

Americans seem to be leading the front against doping in the interest of fair sport. In countries with bigger budgets and interest in biathlon, more than comfortable lives are made from success in the sport and the temptation to acquire a competitive edge to reap the accolades that come with victory is too much for some to handle. Yet elite biathletes like Bailey, who was an elected member of the IBU athletes committee, believed years ago that to compete with the world's best meant adopting ethical training regimens practiced by leading European nations. So whenever there are rogue nations or athletes caught up in impropriety it's no surprise that clean athletes take it personally. Bailey for one called for lifetime bans and higher fines for national federations as he echoes what undoubtedly many of his peers feel. "This is my career, my life, I'm living this 24 hours a day. As an athlete, the idea that I'm competing on a level playing field sustains me."[33]

Epilogue

The state of World Cup biathlon is robust and with the 2026 Milano-Cortina Winter Olympics Games on the horizon, interest in the sport is at an all-time high. Social media platforms across the board have all seen increased activity as the IBU responds to consumer demand for instantaneous and real time information about the sport. Television broadcasting hours over networks such as Eurovision and Eurosport have largely remained stable if not decreased slightly, yet digital media reach, fan engagement, and social media followers has seen steady growth for the past several years. At the 2023 World Championships in Oberhof, Germany, almost 129 million live hours of competition were viewed across ten days with more and more fans turning to video replay platforms to view competitions.[1] And while legends like Ole Einar Bjoerndalen, Martin Fourcade, and Kaisa Makarainen have retired, current stars like JT Boe and Ingrid Landmark Tandrevold will continue to dazzle fans around the globe with their skiing speed and prowess on the shooting range. In Beijing, Norway overtook Germany on the Olympic Games all-time gold and overall medal list. Can we expect from someone in Milano-Cortina a repeat performance of Domracheva, who won three individual competition golds at Sochi in 2018? Is it possible for JT Boe to match Bjoerndalen's tally of three individual gold medals from Salt Lake City in 2002? He came close in Beijing with 2 (sprint and mass start). It remains to be seen but with 61 national federations recognized by the IBU (in full, provisional, or suspended status), victory may soon become more arduous for top nations and biathletes as new talent is discovered in unlikely places.[1,2]

Overlapping with the World Cup schedule in Europe, a series of national biathlon competitions aims to increase exposure and competition in children, youth, and young adults in North America (Canada and the U.S.). The single largest event on the U.S. calendar remains the National Championships, but this year (2024) marks the inaugural U.S. Biathlon Collegiate National Championships which will commence and coincide with the National Championships and highlight the best collegiate athletes and colleges that they attend.[6,7] Much like the rest of the world's sporting events, the COVID-19 pandemic forced the cancellation of many biathlon competitions on the national and world stages potentially hindering development of talent and the sport itself. Thankfully, we seemed to have moved beyond this and full World Cup schedules are published out through 2026 with Lenzerheide (SUI) playing host to the 2025 World Championships on the lead up to the Olympic Winter Games in 2026. Two venues occurring more frequently on the World Cup calendar include Annecy-Le Grand Bornard (FRA) and when viewed from a distance, this Alpine village appears straight out of a Christmas postcard with room to accommodate nearly 10,000 spectators at the biathlon stadium and along the course. Expect the December 2024 sprint race to determine pursuit start times and a mass start race to round out the competition. After former World Cup host Russia lost favor with the IBU following the McLaren Report and recent allegations of corruption with top IBU officials[3], Estonia (Otepaa), with its long cross-country history that has seen remodeling over the years into a modern biathlon facility, has secured a World Cup stop in 2026 with the race schedules yet to be determined.[1,2]

Much anticipation for the upcoming seasons for both fans and athletes alike will be focused on the Antholz-Anterselva (ITA) World Cups as it readies for hosting the 2026 Winter Olympics. This comes some 70 years after Cortina and 20 years following Turin with events taking place from February 6-22, 2026. Will the U.S. win its first biathlon medal on the premier stage of the sport? Despite the challenges of comparably limited resources that U.S. Biathlon faces (much of the 2.9 million dollar budget comes from the United States Olympic Committee and the remaining from in-kind sponsorships and private donations), as opposed to nations like Russia and Norway, in what Max Cobb has described as a "slow-motion start-up", several American biathletes have the potential to podium in Italy. Now under the direction of President and CEO Jack Gierhart who is ready to lead U.S. Biathlon into a new chapter, an organizational restructuring focused on excellence along with a new strategic plan have been undertaken to recognize and develop new talent. Upon moving its headquarters to Midway, UT (Soldier Hollow) efforts begin with John Farra, Director of Sport Development, who hopes to stimulate biathlon participation at a young age through growth of clubs and coaches across the country. Tim Burke then takes over (in actuality a collaborative effort) as the new Director of Athlete Development to progress talent early and ensure that they have the necessary tools and resources to be successful and transition into the senior circuit. Lastly, Lowell Bailey as the Director of High Performance works to fine tune biathletes into potential World Cup and Olympic medalists through training camps and a renewed interest in physiological testing. All this with a strategic goal by 2030 to secure at least one Olympic medal in 2026 and four in 2030; at least one being a coveted gold.[8] In the past, this has forced U.S. Biathlon to adopt an entrepreneurial attitude among its leadership, staff, and athletes, cutting back resources in certain areas to advance others as a means to compete on a global scale against nations that receive far more government/state financial and infrastructure support.[4] As an example, central Norway, along with other regions, offers a high density of sports high schools for students to explore programs that are focused on biathlon for one. The coaches for these programs were almost exclusively all top athletes in their own right, and have access to cutting edge training and/or equipment research coming out of the Norwegian University of Science and Technology

(NTNU). After high school, promising athletes can divide their time between training and coursework at NTNU. Tora Berger and Emil Hegle Svendsen, both Olympic gold medalist biathletes, were products of this system.[5] On the contrary, in the United States many athletes like Susan Dunklee or Grace Castonguay come to biathlon from other endeavors, after demonstrating success in cross-country skiing at the high school or collegiate levels.

The more mature an athlete or the later a talent transfers to biathlon from another sport the greater the challenge; however, with prospects like Castonguay, Kelsey Joan Dickinson, Tara Geraghty-Moats, Amanda Kautzer, Margie Freed, Chloe Levins, Vaclav Cervenka, Vincent Bonacci, Maxime Germain (bronze medalist at the Junior World Championships), and Campbell Wright (gold medalist at the Junior Worlds) alongside veterans Joanne Reid, Deedra Irwin, Jake Brown, Paul Schommer, and Sean Dougherty, a most decorated junior biathlete who arguably just had his best season on the World Cup circuit, this trend may be shifting in the United States. This too might simply be a phenomenon of the sport itself, where more mature biathletes like Martin Fourcade and Lowell Bailey continued to be successful into their mid to late thirties. All said, in the United States athletes come to biathlon in one of three ways; 1) through youth and junior grass roots programs (e.g., Dougherty), 2) after a successful collegiate or other Nordic skiing career (e.g., Dunklee and Freed), and 3) a hybrid model of youth/junior participation, time off for college, and then a return to the sport (e.g., Bailey). U.S. Biathlon hopes to develop and support more coaches across the United States, but for now, relies heavily on volunteers and clubs to help grow and bring interest among youth and parents into the sport. This is no more evident than when past national team athletes upon retirement return to leadership roles at U.S. Biathlon or at other development centers to foster growth in places like Brillion (WI), Craftsbury (VT), Bozeman

(MT), Casper (WY), Bovey (MN), and Soldier Hollow (UT) which should pay dividends in the long term.[4] We've been playing catch up for quite some time, and if recent performances on the World stage prove anything, it's that we as a nation are on the cusp of great results to come.

...

In an auspicious move, the International Biathlon Union has taken over governance of Para Biathlon from the International Paralympic Committee (IPC) and along with the International Ski Federation and Snowboard (FIS) will manage events through a joint steering committee. As IPC President Andrew Parsons said, "IPC and IBU showed a common vision about the future or Para biathlon since the beginning of the discussions about the transfer of governance. We are extremely proud of the work that has been done to develop the sport and the progress achieved while under the governance of the IPC. IBU's commitment to the development and growth of Para biathlon bears testimony to that." IBU President Olle Dahlin added that "we are delighted to have reached this agreement with the IPC, look forward to becoming an IPC member and thank them for their support as we welcome Para biathlon to the IBU family. Growing biathlon and making our sport as accessible as possible are key priorities and bringing Para biathlon under the IBU umbrella is fully aligned with these objectives set out in our strategic plan Target 26 [includes targets of empowering federations, enhancing events, extending reach, upgrading governance, and future innovation]. We are grateful to FIS for their cooperation and look forward to working with them through the Steering Committee to ensure the continued development of Para biathlon around the world." In fact, the IBU recently (2023) held a capacity building forum for developing a "roadmap" to build and grow Para Biathlon focusing on coaching, education, research, and development.[9]

Para Biathlon dates back to Innsbruck in 1988 where it was introduced at the Winter Paralympic Games for athletes with physical impairments. In 1992, the sport was expanded to include athletes with a vision impairment and has been held ever since. Athletes compete in sprint, middle distance, and individual competitions over a 2.0 or 2.5 km course by skiing multiple loops for total distances ranging between 7.5-12.5 km. As with their non-disabled counterparts, biathletes must stop at the shooting range to hit 5 targets at 10 m distance. Miss and there is either a 1-minute penalty or penalty loop to ski; the winner covering the course in the fastest overall time. Athletes with visual impairment are assisted on course with a guide skiing out front who calls out turns. The shooting range itself is divided into two parts with air rifle targets separated from electronic targets. Athletes with a physical impairment shoot pellets at a mechanical target using an air rifle, whereas vision impaired biathletes use an electronic rifle with an infrared camera. When an athlete aims the rifle at a target, acoustic signals are sent to headphones which aid in aiming at the target; changing pitch when the rifle is aimed accurately and on target. Para biathletes do not carry their rifle while skiing but rather are handed one at the range by coaches. Physically impaired athletes may use their own personalized rifles, of course within the rules, while those with visual impairment are provided with standardized rifles which are the same for all individuals. Shooting usually is done in the prone position, however some sit skiers will remain seated if they are unable to shoot prone.[10]

Since the inception of Para Biathlon at the 1988 Winter Paralympics, the United States has been quite successful taking home a total of 14 medals in the various biathlon disciplines achieved by Oksana Masters

TWO SKIS AND A RIFLE: AN INTRODUCTION TO BIATHLON

(2 Gold and 3 Silver), Kendall Gretsch (2 Gold, 1 Silver, and 1 Bronze), Daniel Cnossen (1 Gold and 2 Silver), and Andrew Soule (2 Bronze). Several athletes also compete in Para Nordic Skiing events in conjunction with biathlon and have found similar success at the most elite stage of competition.

...

Having recently returned from volunteering at the 2024 World Cup event at Soldier Hollow in Midway, UT, I can honestly say that none of these events would happen without hundreds of dedicated volunteers, all of whom are fanatical about the sport and freely give their time to ensure smooth and coordinated races. Whether setting up or breaking down the stands, greeting athletes/teams at airports, helping to groom and maintain the race course, recording results on the range which are posted to numerous TV and venue screens, escorting athletes to anti-doping, painting targets between races or zeroing, directing fans, the list goes on and on to make each and every World Cup event run without a hitch. It was a true pleasure and hopefully more than a once in a lifetime experience to have the privilege of volunteering at the Soldier Hollow World Cup held in March 2024 and getting to meet people who are every bit the fan that I am. I can only say thank you for the opportunity. And to my new friends, I hope to see you again!

Image. The author in official IBU volunteer attire standing in front of the shooting range and acquiring a well-earned sunburn during the Soldier Hollow, Utah, USA World Cup held in early March 2024. My primary responsibility was to record missed shots and resultant penalty loop requirements during the women's relay and men's sprint races as a way to cross-check live and automated scoring. (Photo from author's personal archive)

...

TWO SKIS AND A RIFLE: AN INTRODUCTION TO BIATHLON

Go USA and Go Biathlon!

Bibliography and Notes

Chapter One

1. Allen, John B., The Culture and Sport of Skiing. University of Massachusetts Press, August, 2007.
2. Helle, K. Hakon 4 Hakonsson. Norwegian Biographical Lexicon, The Knowledge Agency ANS, February 13, 2009.
3. Killings, Douglas B. & Widger, David. The Project Guttenberg EBook of The Danish History, Books I-IX, by Saxo Grammaticus ("Saxo the Learned"). Release Date: February 11, 2006 [EBook #1150]. Retrieved from: http://www.gutenberg.org/files/1150/1150-h/1150-h.htm.
4. Frank, William D. Everyone to Skis: Skiing in Russia and the rise of Soviet biathlon. Northern Illinois University Press, 2013.
5. Frank, William D. Cold Bullets, Hot Borders: The Shooting War that Russia Won. Skiing Heritage: www.skiingheritage.org, June, 2009.
6. Mattila, Tapani M. maamme turvana [Sea safeguarding our country] (in Finnish). Jyväskylä: K. J. Gummerus Osakeyhtiö, 1983.
7. War on Skis: The Mobile Forces of the North. Publication of the Royal United Services Institute for Defence and Security Studies. 1940. Vol. 85:537, pgs. 103-104.
8. Willmott, Hedley Paul. World War I. New York: Dorling Kindersley, 2003.
9. Henig, Ruth. The Origins of the First World War. Routledge, 2006.
10. Smith, Denis Mack. Modern Italy: A Political History. Ann Arbor: Univ. of Michigan Press, 1997, p. 262.

11. Zehnder, R.D. and Tucker, Spencer C. (Ed.). The European Powers in the First World War: An Encyclopedia. Garland Publishing, Inc. New York & London, 1996.
12. Upton, Anthony F. The Finnish Revolution 1917-1918. University of Minnesota Press, Minneapolis, 1980.
13. Nenye, Vesa, Munter, Peter, Wirtanen, Toni. Finland at War: The Winter War 1939-1940. Osprey Publishing, UK, 2015.
14. Nagorski, Andrew. The Greatest Battle: Stalin, Hitler, and the Desperate Struggle for Moscow That Changed the Course of World War II. Simon & Schuster, 2007.
15. Harper, Frank. Military Ski Manual. Excerpts from the Alpenglow Ski Mountaineering History Project. Published and copyrighted by Skoog, L. www.alpenglow.org, 1943.
16. Mears, Ray. The Real Heroes of Telemark: The true story of the secret mission to stop Hitler's atomic bomb. Hodder and Stoughton, 2003.
17. Odgers, George. Diggers: The Australian Army, Navy, and Air Force in Eleven Years. Landsdowne Publishing, 1994.
18. Shelton, Peter. Climb to Conquer: The Untold Story of WWII's 10th Mountain Division Ski Troops. New York City, New York: Scribner, 2003.
19. Feuer, A.B. Packs On!: Memoirs of the 10th Mountain Division in World War II. Praeger Publishing (1st Edition), 2006.
20. Pennington, Bill. The Legacy of the Soldiers on Skis. New York Times, March 10, 2006.
21. Baghel, Ravi. & Nusser, Marcus. Securing the heights: The vertical dimension of the Siachen conflict between India and Pakistan in the Eastern Karakoram. Elsevier Ltd, 2015. Retrieved from: https://doi.org/10.1016/j.polgeo.2015.05.001.

Chapter Two

1. Heck, Sandra. Von spielenden soldier und kämpfenden Athleten Die Genese des modernen Fünfkamps. Gotingen: V&R Unipress, 2013.
2. Official website of the Olympic Games. www.olympic.org. Retrieved from Modern Pentathlon: https://www.olympic.org/modern-pentathlon
3. Union Internationale de Pentathlon Moderne. Media Guide 2017. Retrieved from: http://www.uipmworld.org/sites/default/files/media_guide_digital_2.pdf
4. Suisse Olympic Committee. General report of the 5th Winter Olympic Games St. Moritz 1948. Retrieved from: http://library.la84.org/6oic/OfficialReports/1948/ORW1948.pdf
5. Mallon, Bill & Heijmans, Jeroen. Historical Dictionary of the Olympic Movement (4th Edition). Scarecrow Press, Inc., 2011.
6. Stegen, Art. Biathlon. National Rifle Association of America, 1979.
7. Official website of the Olympic Games. www.olympic.org. Retrieved from results database: https://www.olympic.org/chamonix-1924/military-patrol/military-patrol-men
8. Suisse Olympic Committee. Report of the Olympic Games St, Moritz 1928. Retrieved from: http://www.la84foundation.org/6oic/OfficialReports/1928/1928w2.pdf
9. German Olympic Committee. Report of the Olympic Games Garmisch-Partenkirchen 1936. Retrieved from: http://www.la84foundation.org/6oic/OfficialReports/1936/1936win.pdf
10. Official website of the Patrouille des Glaciers. www.pdg.ch/

en/welcome/. Retrieved from history: www.pdg.ch/en/lapdg/history/

11. Frank, William D. Everyone to Skis: Skiing in Russia and the rise of Soviet biathlon. Northern Illinois University Press, 2013. The reader is strongly encouraged to consult this resource for great historical and geopolitical detail on subsequent world biathlon championships.

12. *Kunnskapsforlagets idrettsleksikon* (Encyclopedia of Sports). Oslo: Kunnskapsforlaget, 1990.

13. Extract of the minutes of the 55th session of the International Olympic Committee, Munich, Germany, May 25-29, 1959. Retrieved from: http://library.la84.org/OlympicInformationCenter/OlympicReview/1959/BDCE67/BDCE67zb.pdf

14. Modern Pentathlon, Biathlon, and Olympism. A document prepared by the UIPM in 1983. Retrieved from: http://library.la84.org/OlympicInformationCenter/OlympicReview/1983/ore192/ORE192zc.pdf

15. Official website of Biathlon Canada. www.biathloncanada.ca. Retrieved from history of biathlon: http://biathloncanada.ca/learn-about-biathlon/history-of-biathlon/

16. California Olympic Commission, Rubin, R. (Ed). Final report of the 8th Olympic Winter Games, 1960. Retrieved from: http://library.la84.org/6oic/OfficialReports/1960/1960w.pdf

17. Wallechinsky, David. The complete book of the Winter Olympics. The Overlook Press, Woodstock & New York, 1998.

18. Official website of the International Biathlon Union. www.biathlonworld.com. Retrieved from history 1973-1978: http://ibu-update.swhosting10.de/en/history_1973_1978.html

19. Official website of the International Biathlon Union. www.biathlonworld.com. Retrieved from datacenter: biathlonresults.com
20. Official website of the International Biathlon Union. www.biathlonworld.com. Retrieved from history 1979-1994: http://ibu-update.swhosting10.de/en/history_1979_1994.html
21. French Olympic Committee. Official report of the XVI Olympic Winter Games of Albertville and Savoie, 1992. Retrieved from: http://library.la84.org/6oic/OfficialReports/1992/orw1992.pdf
22. Official website of the International Biathlon Union. www.biathlonworld.com. Retrieved from: https://www.biathlonworld.com/about-biathlon/#history
23. Official website of United States Biathlon. www.usbiathlon.org. Retrieved from: http://www.usbiathlon.org/history.html
24. Official website of the International Biathlon Union. www.biathlonworld.com. Retrieved from: https://www.biathlon-antholz.it/en/world-cup-2024/short-individual-men/15-409.html
25. The official website of the International Biathlon Union. https://www.biathlonworld.com/inside-ibu/downloads/. Retrieved from: https://assets.ctfassets.net/cz0vl36hcq0x/7mkQn1kQTB7VzlUZHAcuec/7fee90904a77b43c4b0346ceb1c54704/Rules_2023-11_EN_cap3.pdf.

Chapter Three

1. SMHI Monthly Data 2002-2015. Retrieved from: http://www.smhi.se/klimatdata/meteorologi/temperatur/

2.1240
2. The official website of the International Biathlon Union. Retrieved from news and media: http://ibu-update.swhosting10.de/en/press_releases.html/do/detail?presse=676
3. Website of Ostersund Biathlon Competition. Retrieved from: http://www.worldcupostersund.se/content/uploads/2016/06/Nykarta.pdf
4. The official website of the International Biathlon Union. http://www.biathlonworld.com/downloads/. Retrieved from: https://assets.ctfassets.net/cz0vl36hcq0x/7mkQn1kQTB7VzlUZHAcuec/7fee90904a77b43c4b0346ceb1c54704/Rules_2023-11_EN_cap3.pdf.
5. Official website of the International Biathlon Union. www.biathlonworld.com. Retrieved from datacenter: biathlonresults.com.
6. Biathlon Pokljuka website. http://www.biathlon-pokljuka.com/BIATHLON_POKLJUKA_EN,,svetovni_pokal.htm. Retrieved from: http://www.biathlon-pokljuka.com/BIATHLON_POKLJUKA_EN,,o_pokljuki.htm.
7. Biathlon Pokljuka website. http://www.biathlon-pokljuka.com/BIATHLON_POKLJUKA_EN,,svetovni_pokal.htm. Retrieved from: http://www.biathlon-pokljuka.com/files/02_SVETOVNI_POKAL/DECEMBER-2016/INFO-za-tekmovalce/official-invitation-bwc-pokljuka-2016.pdf.
8. Biathlon Nove Mesto Website. Retrieved from: http://www.vysocina-arena.cz/en/arrival-at-nmnm.html.
9. Website for the Oberhof World Cup. https://www.weltcup-oberhof.com/. Retrieved from: https://www.weltcup-

oberhof.com/world-cup/on-the-spot/dkb-ski-arena/.
10. Website for the Ruhpolding World Cup. https://www.biathlon-ruhpolding.de/en. Retrieved from: https://www.biathlon-ruhpolding.de/en/weltcup-2018/chiemgau-arena
11. Website for Antholz-Anterselva World Cup. http://www.biathlon-antholz.it/EN/mappa-stadio.php#. Retrieved from Venue/stadium: http://www.biathlon-antholz.it/images/mappa-stadio.jpg
12. Biathlon World. A publication of the International Biathlon Union. The World of Biathlon, Personalities, Events, Results Season Review, 2017, Vol. 43.
13. A Eurovision Sports broadcast. Posted by T&F Boss. Video of the 2017 Men's Individual World Championship race, Published on February 16, 2017. Retrieved from: https://www.youtube.com/watch?v=jc44PIdg7iE.
14. Little, Chelsea. Transcendent on the shooting range, Dunklee claims World Champs silver. www.fasterskier.com, February 19, 2017. Retrieved from: http://fasterskier.com/fsarticle/transcendant-shooting-range-dunklee-claims-world-champs-silver/.
15. Fasterskier. Notes and quotes: Pyeongchang biathlon World Cups. www.fasterskier.com, March 6, 2017. Retrieved from: http://fasterskier.com/fsarticle/notes-quotes-pyeongchang-biathlon-world-cups/.
16. Butler, Nick. Kontiolahti in Finland replaces Tyumen in Russia as host of IBU World Cup event. www.insidethegamesbiz.com, January 7, 2017. Retrieved from: https://www.insidethegames.biz/articles/1045549/kontiolahti-in-finland-replaces-tyumen-in-russia-as-host-of-ibu-world-cup-event.
17. Burke, Patrick. Work on Milano Cortina 2026 Biathlon

venue paused with call for tenders to be relaunched. July 8, 2023. Retrieved from: https://www.insidethegames.biz/articles/1138730/south-tyrol-arena-mc-2026-delays.

Chapter Four

1. The official website of the International Biathlon Union. https://www.biathlonworld.com/inside-ibu/downloads/. Retrieved from: https://assets.ctfassets.net/cz0vl36hcq0x/7mkQn1kQTB7VzlUZHAcuec/7fee90904a77b43c4b0346ceb1c54704/Rules_2023-11_EN_cap3.pdf
2. Official website of the International Biathlon Union. www.biathlonworld.com. Retrieved from datacenter: biathlonresults.com.
3. Zimmer, Harald. Fourcade wins despite ammo flub: 'Squirrel drama' in women's mass start in Oslo. www.fasterskier.com, March 19, 2017. Retrieved from: http://fasterskier.com/fsarticle/fourcade-wins-despite-ammo-flub-squirrel-drama-womens-mass-start-oslo/.
4. Website of the US Biathlon Association. http://www.teamusa.org/US-Biathlon. Retrieved from: http://www.teamusa.org/US-Biathlon/Team-and-Hall-of-Fame/Staff-and-Coaches.
5. Morton, John. Aiming for Victory. Vermont has bred some of the nation's best biathletes. Published by Vermont Sports. www.vtsports.com, December 1, 2011. Retrieved from: http://vtsports.com/aiming-for-victory-vermont-has-bred-some-of-the-nations-best-biathletes/.
6. Olympic Team Norway. Team and Media Guide, Sochi, 2014. Retrieved from: http://www.olympiatoppen.no/om_olympiatoppen/aktuelt/media41483.media.

7. Olympic Winter Games Team USA Media Guide, 2014. Retrieved from: www.teamusa.org/-/media/TeamUSA/ForTheMedia/2014-Team-USA-Media-Guide.pdf.
8. *Website of the US Biathlon Association. Financial Statement, June 30, 2022 and 2021.* Retrieved from:https://assets.contentstack.io/v3/assets/blteb7d012fc7ebef7f/blt03d469d6f48f5a62/646c084b6bb6f7816fe87537/United_States_Biathlon_Association_FS.pdf.
9. Costantini, Lisa. 5 Things You Didn't Know about Biathlon. Published by the Website of Team USA, www.teamusa.org, Dec. 22, 2016. Retrieved from: http://www.teamusa.org/News/2016/December/22/5-Things-You-Didnt-Know-About-Biathlon.
10. Molon, Adam. How do you get to Sochi? Land a big-deal sponsor. Published by NBC News, www.nbcnews.com, February 6, 2014. Retrieved from: https://www.nbcnews.com/storyline/sochi-olympics/how-do-you-get-sochi-land-big-deal-sponsor-n23921.
11. Becker, Lars. World Cup Heroine from Hochfilzen on sponsors, TV presence, and social media. www.ispo.com, February 22, 2017. Retrieved from: http://www.ispo.com/en/people/id_79703182/laura-dahlmeier-you-earn-good-money-from-biathlons-.html.
12. Official website of Magdalena Neuner. http://www.magdalena-neuner.de/. Retrieved from: http://www.magdalena-neuner.de/about/.
13. Zaccardi, Nick. Ole Einar Bjoerndalen: 'Boring' biathlete also greatest Olympian you've never heard of. www.nbc.sports.com, February 9, 2014. Retrieved from: http://olympics.nbcsports.com/2014/02/09/ole-einar-bjoerndalen-boring-biathlete-also-greatest-unknown-

olympian/.
14. Official website of the Olympic Games. www.olympic.org. Retrieved from: https://www.olympic.org/ole-einar-bjoerndalen.
15. Net Industries. Sports.jrank.org. Retrieved from: http://sports.jrank.org/pages/1516/Forsberg-Magdalena-Career-Change.html.
16. Butler, Nick. Swedish biathlon star to feature in Eurosport PyeongChang 2018 coverage. www.insidethegamesbi.com, March 22, 2017. Retrieved from: https://www.insidethegames.biz/articles/1048436/swedish-biathlon-star-to-feature-in-eurosport-pyeongchang-2018-coverage.
17. Little, Chelsea. For Fourcade, cross-country was worth a try – Now back to biathlon. www.fasterskier.com, November 28, 2012. Retrieved from: http://fasterskier.com/fsarticle/for-fourcade-cross-country-was-worth-a-try-now-back-to-biathlon/.
18. Real Biathlon. www.realbiathlon.com, Posted March 26, 2016. Retrieved from: http://www.realbiathlon.com/2016/03/201516-top-skiers-men.html.
19. Willemsen, Eric. Fourcade wins gold in men's 12.5km pursuit in Sochi. Associated Press, February 10, 2014. Retrieved from: http://wintergames.ap.org/article/fourcade-wins-gold-mens-125k-pursuit-sochi.
20. Zimmer, Harald. Fourcade matches Poirée's record Burke climbs to seventh; Pfeiffer suffers concussion. www.fasterskier.com, February 12, 2016. Retrieved from: http://fasterskier.com/fsarticle/fourcade-matches-poiree-with-44th-win-burke-climbs-to-seventh-peiffers-scary-crash-in-pursuit/.
21. Frank, William D. Everyone to skis! Skiing in Russia and the

rise of Soviet biathlon. Northern Illinois University Press, 2013, Quote from p. 231.
22. Real Biathlon. All-time records men. www.realbiathlon.com, Updated March 20, 2016. Retrieved from: http://www.realbiathlon.com/p/all-time-records-men.html.
23. Kilner, James. Life as usual for Russia boss guilty of murder plot. www.washingtonpost.com, August 8, 2007. Retrieved from: http://www.washingtonpost.com/wp-dyn/content/article/2007/08/08/AR2007080801399.html.
24. Official website of the Olympic Games. www.olympic.org. Retrieved from: https://www.olympic.org/uschi-disl.
25. Official website of Rossignol skis. www.rossignol.com. Retrieved from: http://www.rossignol.com/US/US/news—56ob3yo04nem.html.
26. Official website of the Olympic Games. www.olympic.org. Retrieved from: https://www.olympic.org/news/norwegian-tora-berger-is-seeking-golden-finale-in-sochi.
27. Real biathlon. www.realbiathlon.com, Updated March 17, 2013. Retrieved from: http://www.realbiathlon.com/2012/02/is-tora-berger-in-shape-for-world.html.
28. Bouchez, Yann. Raphael Poirée: The bipatride. www.lemonde.fr, March 3, 2016. Retrieved from: http://www.lemonde.fr/sports-de-glisse/visuel/2016/03/03/on-a-retrouve-raphael-poiree_4875627_1616666.html.
29. Real biathlon. Raphael Poirée career. www.realbiathlon.com, Posted November 7, 2012. Retrieved from: http://www.realbiathlon.com/2012/11/raphael-poiree-career-review.html.
30. Official website of the Olympic Games. www.olympic.org. Retrieved from: https://www.olympic.org/news/women-s-biathlon-indomitable-domracheva-lands-golden-treble.
31. Official website of the International Biathlon Union.

www.biathlonworld.com. November 24, 2022. Retrieved from https://www.biathlonworld.com/news/bi18-institutional-rule-changes/IC2xOiQt6bhRKSWm1uZwt.
32. Official website of the International Biathlon Union. www.biathlonworld.com. Retrieved from https://www.biathlonworld.com/news/detail/ole-and-darya-coaching-the-chinese-team.
33. NBC Sports. Retrieved from https://olympics.nbcsports.com/2020/03/13/martin-fourcade-retires-biathlon/.
34. Official website of the International Biathlon Union. www.biathlonworld.com. Retrieved from https://www.biathlonworld.com/news/detail/ibu-magazine-55.
35. Focus Biathlon: Biathlon News. This is Madness! The Norwegians send Christiansen to the IBU Cup, exchanging him for Botn. December 20, 2023. Retrieved from: https://focusbiathlon.com/news/item/930-this-is-madness-the-norwegians-send-christiansen-to-the-ibu-cup-exchanging-him-for-botn.html.
36. U.S. Biathlon. October 26, 2023. Long-time U.S. Biathlon Coach, Mentor, Supporter Algis Shalna Announces Retirement. Retrieved from: https://www.usbiathlon.org/news/2023/october/26/long-time-u-s-biathlon-coach-mentor-supporter-algis-shalna-announces-retirement.

Chapter Five

1. Official website of the Olympic Games. www.olympic.org. Retrieved from: https://www.olympic.org/cross-country-skiing-equipment-and-history.
2. Huntford, Roland. Two Planks and a Passion: The dramatic

history of skiing. Published by Continuum, 2008.
3. Lund, Morten. & Masia, Seth. A Short History of Skis. www.skiinghistory.org, (n.d.). Retrieved from: https://www.skiinghistory.org/history/short-history-skis-0.
4. Frank, William D. Everyone to skis! Skiing in Russia and the rise of Soviet biathlon. Northern Illinois University Press, 2013.
5. Masia, Seth. Grip and Glide. Skiing Heritage, 2010, 22(2): 42-45. Other manufacturers of wax (Swix) include Toko, Holmenkol, Maplus, and Rex. Quote from page 44.
6. Bengtsson, Bengt Erik. Cross-country skating: How it all started. www.skiinghistory.org, (n.d.). Retrieved from: https://www.skiinghistory.org/history/cross-country-skating-how-it-started.
7. The official website of the International Biathlon Union. www.biathlonworld.com, http://www.biathlonworld.com/downloads/. Retrieved from: http://res.cloudinary.com/deltatre-spa-ibu/image/upload/zfrykee6evqyz4lteurb.pdf *and* http://res.cloudinary.com/deltatre-spa-ibu/image/upload/otzjvphra5dxsmpqknd7.pdf.
8. United States Ski and Snowboard Association. Cross Country Technique Fundamentals. V2 Alternate. www.tsaltwshi.org, 2006. Retrieved from: http://www.tsalteshi.org/wp-content/uploads/2011/04/Us-ski-team-skate-v2-alternate.pdf.
9. Real biathlon. Fastest Skiers Statistics for Men and Women. www.realbiathlon.com. Retrieved from: http://www.realbiathlon.com/2016/03/201516-top-skiers-men.html and http://www.realbiathlon.com/2016/03/201516-top-skiers-women.html.
10. Muha, Mike. Nordic Integrated System. www.nordicskiracer.com, January 26, 2005. Retrieved from:

http://www.nordicskiracer.com/Equipment/2005/NIS/NIS.asp.
11. Brooker, Kevin. How it's made: Base material. www.fasterskier.com, February 11, 2009. Retrieved from: http://fasterskier.com/fsarticle/how-its-made-base-material/.
12. Brown, Nat. The Complete Guide to Cross-Country Ski Preparation. Published by The Mountaineers, 2005. Remains perhaps the most comprehensive resource on cross-country ski wax and preparation. Quote from page 109.
13. International Biathlon Union. IBU TV: The Science of the Wax, February 4, 2017. Retrieved from: https://www.youtube.com/watch?v=xtv83XJ9EmU.
14. Breitschadel, Felix. Variation of Nordic Classic Ski Characteristics from Norwegian national team athletes. Procedia Engineering, 2012, 34: 391-396.
15. Albert, Jason. US Biathlon's Clare Egan: Calm, Cool, and on the Rise. www.fasterskier.com, December 8, 2016. Retrieved from: http://fasterskier.com/fsarticle/us-biathlons-clare-egan-calm-cool-and-on-the-rise/.
16. Fasterskier. FIS Moves to Ban Fluorinated Ski Waxes for the 2020/2021 Season, November 23, 2019. Retrieved from: https://fasterskier.com/fsarticle/fis-moves-to-ban-fluorinated-ski-waxes-for-the-2020-2021-season/.
17. International Biathlon Union. March 22, 2023. IBU Implements full fluor ban. Retrieved from: https://www.biathlonworld.com/news/ibu-full-fluor-ban/4XFVREtVcQrtG7cd4nHhxp.
18. Spotify Podcast. November 2023. Fede Fontana: Farwell to Fluorocarbons. Retrieved from: https://open.spotify.com/episode/7nFkFX0cLVPytUHLloyYTl?si=4Ts7K94ISoKzhbwZytVnfg&nd=

19. International Biathlon Union. Fluor Test Protocols for IBU Events. Retrieved from: https://assets.ctfassets.net/cz0vl36hcq0x/38vAOJPXKXuPxNtkRrPUNa/ebf2129f281cee18c291570abd1a126e/Fluor_test_protocol_for_IBU_Events_V.1.0_2023-24.pdf.

Chapter Six

1. Official website of JGA Anschutz. Retrieved from: http://jga.anschuetz-sport.com/index.php5?produktID=267&menu=99&sprache=1&produktS.
2. Bracholdt, Claudia. This German invention is used in 95% of rifles in biathlon. Quartz Media, LLC, February 16, 2013. Retrieved from: https://qz.com/54254/this-german-invention-is-used-in-95-of-rifles-in-biathlons/.
3. The official website of the International Biathlon Union. www.biathlonworld.com. https://www.biathlonworld.com/inside-ibu/downloads. Retrieved from: https://assets.ctfassets.net/cz0vl36hcq0x/2iDuPyE16smAkjo3DoobKs/7a20527ee03844e48d05612cd2e6a4a2/Rules_2023-08_EN_cap4.pdf. Other manufacturers of biathlon targets include Kurvinen (FIN), Devon (USA), AccuPro (CAN), VingMek (NOR), and Megalink (NOR).
4. USA Biathlon. U.S. Biathlon Association Coaches' Education, 2016. Retrieved from: https://www.anchoragenordicski.com/wp-content/uploads/2016/08/CoachesEducation.pdf.
5. Team Great Britain. Olympic biathlon rifle explained by team GB's Amanda Lightfoot. Published on January 29, 2014. Retrieved from: https://www.youtube.com/watch?v=7HZUTV4F9Js.

6. Dunklee, Susan. Stock Stories. Published on August 1, 2013. Retrieved from: https://susandunklee.wordpress.com/page/4/.
7. Official website of Eley ammunition. Eley tennex biathlon – 01400. Retrieved from: http://www.eley.co.uk/eley-tenex-biathlon. Biathlon ammunition is also supplied by the Lapua company.
8. International Biathlon Union. IBU Rules for Advertising 2022-2026. Retrieved from: https://assets.ctfassets.net/cz0vl36hcq0x/14iWpe4GzRSo5AriVAwIht/4f85ed76ab5a5a75808629b873a6a950/02082023_IBU_Advertising_Rules_2022-2026.pdf.
9. Little, Chelsea. Transcendent on the shooting range, Dunklee claims World Champs silver. www.fasterskier.com, February 19, 2017. Retrieved from: http://fasterskier.com/fsarticle/transcendant-shooting-range-dunklee-claims-world-champs-silver/.
10. Official website of the International Biathlon Union. www.biathlonworld.com. Retrieved from datacenter: biathlonresults.com.
11. Real biathlon. 2023-2024 Season Statistics. www.realbiathlon.com. Retrieved from: https://www.realbiathlon.com/seasons.html?gender=M&category=shootingTimes and https://www.realbiathlon.com/seasons.html?gender=W&category=shootingTimes.
12. International Biathlon Union. June 29, 2021. New rifles for the new season. Retrieved from: https://www.biathlonworld.com/news/new-rifles-new-season/9DmYZ57w30Gt4B5pD3HfQ.

Chapter Seven

1. Losnegard, Thomas. Physiological determinants of performance in modern elite cross-country skiing. Dissertation from the Norwegian School of Sports Sciences, 2013. Retrieved from: https://brage.bibsys.no/xmlui/bitstream/handle/11250/171349/Losnegard2013.pdf?sequence=1.
2. Holmberg, Hans-Christer. The elite cross-country skier provides unique insights into human exercise physiology. Scandinavian Journal of Medicine & Science in Sports, 2015, Vol. 25: Supplement S4, 100-109. Retrieved from: http://onlinelibrary.wiley.com/doi/10.1111/sms.12601/full.
3. Tonnesson, E., Haugen, T.A., Hem, E., Leirstein, S, and Seiler, S. Maximal aerobic capacity in the Winter-Olympics endurance disciplines: Olympic-medal benchmarks for the time period 1990-2013. International Journal of Sports Physiology and Performance, 2015, Vol. 10, 835-839.
4. Egan, Clare. One year done, another begun. Published on May 18, 2017. Retrieved from: https://clareegan.wordpress.com/2017/05/.
5. Dunklee, Susan. A week with the international biathlon team. Published on July 27, 2015. Retrieved from: https://susandunklee.wordpress.com/.
6. Egan, Clare. A window into training camp psyche. Published on October 24, 2013. Retrieved from: http://greenracingproject.com/blog/5019/a-window-into-training-camp-psyche/. An excellent resource for biathlete blogs and race reports.
7. International Biathlon Union. Lithuanians alone on a quiet day in Obertilliach. www.biathlonworld.com, September 11, 2017. Retrieved from: http://www.biathlonworld.com/

news/detail/lithuanians-alone-on-a-quiet-day-in-obertilliach.

8. International Biathlon Union. Coaches' Corner: Italy's Patrick Oberegger. www.biathlonworld.com, September 6, 2017. Retrieved from: http://www.biathlonworld.com/news/detail/coaches-corner-italy-s-patrick-oberegger.

9. Official website of Schnals Senales: The glacier area. Biathlon training at the Val Senales Glacier in South Tyrol: Perfect conditions for high altitude training. www.schnalstal.com. Retrieved from: http://www.schnalstal.com/en/training-center/high-altitude-training/biathlon.html.

10. Official website of DKB-Skisport-Halle Oberhof. http://www.oberhof-skisporthalle.de/en/. Retrieved from: http://www.oberhof-skisporthalle.de/en/skihalle/facts-and-figures/.

11. International Biathlon Union. Some like it cold: Kontiolahti ice swimming. www.biathlonworld.com, March 13, 2017. Retrieved from: http://www.biathlonworld.com/news/detail/some-like-it-cold-kontiolahti-ice-swimming.

12. USA Biathlon. U.S. Biathlon Association Coaches' Education, 2016. Retrieved from: https://www.anchoragenordicski.com/wp-content/uploads/2016/08/CoachesEducation.pdf.

13. Price, Karen. With Olympic champion shooter Matt Emmons' help, the US Biathlon Team is on target for 2018. www.teamusa.org, March 16, 2017. Retrieved from: https://www.teamusa.org/News/2017/March/16/With-Olympic-Champion-Shooter-Matt-Emmons-Help-The-US-Biathlon-Team-Is-On-Target-For-2018.

14. Dunklee, Susan. In the Mix. Published on March 2, 2014. Retrieved from: https://susandunklee.wordpress.com/page/2/.

15. Oyvind Skattebo and Thomas Losnegard. Variability,

Predictability and Race Factors Affecting Performance in Elite Biathlon. International Journal of Sports Physiology and Performance, (in press) accepted for publication June 15, 2017. Retrieved from: http://journals.humankinetics.com/doi/pdf/10.1123/ijspp.2017-0090.
16. Hall, Zach. Cleaning your biathlon rifle. Published on January 13, 2014. Retrieved from: https://www.youtube.com/watch?v=sWSHYNJcDPw.
17. International Biathlon Union. IBU Biathlon Guide 2017/2018. www.biathlonworld.com, October 9, 2017. Retrieved from: http://res.cloudinary.com/deltatre-spa-ibu/image/upload/ovep9c9reko6njwhbceq.
18. Frank, William D. Everyone to Skis: Skiing in Russia and the rise of Soviet biathlon. Northern Illinois University Press, 2013.
19. Waddington, Ivan & Smith, Andy. An introduction to drugs in sport: Addicted to winning? Routledge Taylor & Francis Group, London and New York, 2009.
20. John Underwood. Interview for ABC Sports by Mike Adamle, February 20, 1988. Details from quote in Frank, W.D. Everyone to Skis: Skiing in Russia and the rise of Soviet biathlon. Northern Illinois University Press, 2013, p. 258.
21. Wallechinsky, David. The complete book of the Winter Olympics. The Overlook Press, Woodstock & New York, 1998.
22. Kelso, Paul. Six Austrian Nordic skiers banned for life by IOC for blood-doping. The Guardian, April 25, 2007. Retrieved from: https://www.theguardian.com/sport/2007/apr/26/sport.sport.
23. Little, Chelsea. IBU hands down doping bans for three Russians in re-testing cases. www.fasterskier.com, July 13, 2015. Retrieved from: http://fasterskier.com/fsarticle/ibu-

hands-down-doping-bans-for-three-russians-in-re-testing-cases/.

24. Ruiz, Rebecca & Schwirtz, Michael. Russian insider says state-run doping fueled Olympic gold. The New York Times, May 12, 2016. Retrieved from: https://www.nytimes.com/2016/05/13/sports/russia-doping-sochi-olympics-2014.html.

25. McLaren, Richard. Independent person WADA investigation of Sochi allegations. Report submitted to WADA, July 16, 2016. Retrieved from: https://www.wada-ama.org/sites/default/files/resources/files/20160718_ip_report_newfinal.pdf.

26. The Associated Press report published by USA Today. Biathlon body clears 22 Russians, investigating 7 others. www.usatoday.com, January 21, 2017. Retrieved from: https://www.usatoday.com/story/sports/olympics/2017/01/21/biathlon-body-clears-22-russians-investigating-7-others/96893148/.

27. Fasterskier. WADA dismisses cases of 95 Russian athletes. www.fasterskier.com, September 15, 2017. Retrieved from: http://blogs.fasterskier.com/doping/2017/09/15/wada-dismisses-cases-of-95-russian-athletes/.

28. United States Anti-Doping Agency. Doping crisis threatens 2018 Winter Olympic Games. www.usada.org, September 14, 2017. Retrieved from: https://www.usada.org/doping-crisis-threatens-2018-winter-olympic-games/.

29. Dunklee, Susan. A one week break, Bavarian style. Published on February 4, 2015. Retrieved from: https://susandunklee.wordpress.com/.

30. International Biathlon Union. Integrity Code. www.biathlonworld.com. http://www.biathlonworld.com/downloads/. Retrieved from: http://res.cloudinary.com/

31. RIA. Латание мышиных дыр тестом: эксперт о допинговом скандале со сборной Казахстана. February 9, 2017. Retrieved from: https://riafan.ru/609040-lataniemyshinyh-dyr-testom-ekspert-o-dopingovom-skandale-so-sbornoi-kazahstana.
32. Little, Chelsea. What about TUE's? The counterpoint to doping scandals, and rarely granted in biathlon. www.fasterskier.com, February 20, 2017. Retrieved from: http://fasterskier.com/fsarticle/tues-counterpoint-doping-scandals-rarely-granted-biathlon/.
33. Powell, Michael. Winter sports athletes ask for the doping spotlight. The New York Times, March 29, 2016. Retrieved from: https://www.nytimes.com/2016/03/30/sports/pervasive-doping-in-summer-sports-is-likely-only-the-half-of-it.html.
34. International Biathlon Union. IBU makes important calendar and sports decisions amid Congress preparations, June 11, 2019. Retrieved from: https://www.biathlonworld.com/news/detail/ibu-makes-important-calendar-and-sports-decisions-amid-congress-preparations.
35. Sattlecker, G., Edfelder, J., and Gressenbauer, C. (2018). International Biathlon Union. Exercise Catalogue for Biathlon Shooting. Retrieved from: https://assets.ctfassets.net/cz0vl36hcq0x/1yIzeQwKuz9YM1fysHCbXA/45fea0394d3ce748a74e40edd284dfc8/kfgfyxepc9l5om9vdebz.pdf.
36. International Biathlon Union. Russian Biathlon Union Reinstatement Criteria. Retrieved from: https://assets.ctfassets.net/cz0vl36hcq0x/

k1zVZmJLp0S3VojGK1Wy1g/
e30f69b6a3ff21d2e7eab553b63b8cbe/
Russian_Biathlon_Union_Reinstatement_Criteria_18122018.pdf.

Epilogue

1. International Biathlon Union. IBU Biathlon Guide 2023-2024. www.biathlonworld.com. Retrieved from: https://downloads.ctfassets.net/cz0vl36hcq0x/3L1Ssh969Y1bVuToZe9B3G/235e32b52e24f328fb836f66ff4e82c8/IBUGuide2024_Digital.pdf.
2. Olympedia. Retrieved from: https://www.olympedia.org/sports/BTH.
3. Etchells, Daniel. Inside the Games. International Biathlon Union makes move to help tackle doping. June 12, 2019. Retrieved from: https://www.insidethegames.biz/articles/1080494/international-biathlon-union-makes-move-to-help-tackle-doping.
4. Albert, Jason. Nordic Nation: Max Cobb, US Biathlon's Straight Shooter. www.fasterskier.com, October 18, 2017. Podcast interview by Jason Albert of Max Cobb on September 8, 2017. Retrieved from: http://fasterskier.com/fsarticle/nordic-nation-max-cobb-us-biathlons-straight-shooter/.
5. Norwegian University of Science and Technology. Norway's winning Olympic Recipe. www.ntnu.edu, January 3, 2010. Retrieved from: https://www.ntnu.edu/news/olympic-recipe.
6. U.S. Biathlon. National Events and Camps. Retrieved from: https://www.usbiathlon.org/national-events-calendar.
7. U.S. Biathlon. U.S. Biathlon Collegiate National

Championships. Retrieved from: https://www.usbiathlon.org/us-biathlon-collegiate-national-championships.
8. U.S. Biathlon. U.S. Biathlon Strategic Plan 2030. Retrieved from: https://www.usbiathlon.org/about-us/strategic-plan.
9. International Paralympic Committee. IPC transfers governance of Para biathlon to IBU, July 13, 2022. Retrieved from: https://www.paralympic.org/news/ipc-transfers-governance-para-biathlon-ibu.
10. International Biathlon Union. About Para Biathlon. Retrieved from: https://www.paralympic.org/news/ipc-transfers-governance-para-biathlon-ibu.

www.ingramcontent.com/pod-product-compliance
Ingram Content Group UK Ltd.
Pitfield, Milton Keynes, MK11 3LW, UK
UKHW020707041225
9370UKWH00046B/1095